A GUIDE TO BUGLING BULLS

How to Conquer 14 Tough Challenges In Life

PAUL N. CARLSON

ISBN: 978-1-63443-803-2

DEDICATION

I dedicate this book…

… to my dad, who sowed the first seeds of a love of hunting and God's great outdoors in me when I was a boy. My first remembrance of hunting is walking through tall cornfields in my home state of Minnesota in search of pheasants. Even at that early age I was starting to understand that hunting was more about who we were with than what we were after. And Dad gave me a holy love and reverence for the God who created the heavens and the earth.

… and to all the sportsmen who are passionate about discovering all the hidden mysteries of the majestic elk. This book is for those who are not content with hiring somebody else to do all their homework for them but are committed to learning to "do-it-yourself." It's for those who want to share their journey with a child, family member, or friend. And it's for those who have a sense of awe for God's great outdoors and the wildlife that are such a great treasure in North America.

CONTENTS

ACKNOWLEDGMENTS

My personal thanks goes first of all to my wife, Ruth, who supported and helped me in my endeavors to hunt elk for over thirty years and to get the most out of God's great outdoors. She encouraged me to write this book and helped with editing. I want to thank my son, Jonathan, who helped me with editing, proofreading, establishing a website, and solving many problems. He is my "Go-to-guy."

I also want to thank all the guys in this book with whom I have had the joy of hunting and from whom I learned so much. We hunted, laughed, and celebrated together, we shared frustrations and disappointments together, and we encouraged each other to keep going in tough times. We shared expenses, vehicles, trailers, tents, and other necessary equipment, and we pitched in together to get to Colorado to make our do-it-yourself adventures possible.

My personal thanks also goes to Steve Sorensen, who showed me how to decide on the right format for the book, lay it out, and keep the typography consistent. He also proofread the script and answered many questions.

Finally, I owe so much to Ray Mehrer, who took me on my first elk hunts in Wyoming, taught me some of the basics of hunting elk, and showed me how to take care of and process the harvest.

INTRODUCTION

My love for elk hunting began in 1981 when my wife, Ruth, and I moved from Minnesota to Colorado to pastor a small church in the northeastern plateau area. We were a long way from the mountains, but I recall watching the news reports of hunters making their way up into the beautiful Rocky Mountains to try to harvest one of these giant animals. Somehow a seed of interest in knowing more about this big game animal and being able to spend extended time in this majestic country was planted in my heart.

In 1982, we moved to north central Wyoming to work on staff at a church in the Bighorn Basin, and it was there that I had my first experience with elk hunting. I was invited by Ray Mehrer, the Senior Pastor, an avid and successful elk hunter, to go with him into his camp where he shared with me his love for the country and elk.

These memories are still etched in my mind, and I can even see those magnificent Bighorn Mountains, the elk that seemed to mystically appear from the timber into the meadows, and the first elk we downed. I approached it and was immediately overwhelmed at the size of the animal and asked, "What are we going to do with that huge thing?" We moved to northeast Wisconsin in 1985, and I have continued to take trips back to Colorado and the high country to satisfy my love for this adventure.

One day, as I was looking for a way to avoid hunting crowds and learn more about this animal, I ran into some information about a special season for muzzleloaders. I have bow hunted for whitetail deer ever since I was in high school, but using a bow for elk seemed like an impossible feat because of the vast size of the country and the thickness of the timber. But here was a season in September, during the changing of the aspen colors, during the bugling season, with far fewer hunters where we could use a gun. I would still get up close and personal with the elk, but I'd have a much better chance of success than with a bow! I asked one of my hunting buddies from our church what he thought about hunting elk with muzzleloaders, and before long we were buying "smoke poles" and learning the rules of a new challenge that we soon loved.

I still remember our first muzzleloader hunt in the White River National Forest of Colorado. There were five of us, and you'll meet each man within the pages of this book. We made our camp about two miles up an old logging road in a meadow that bordered a wilderness area. We had few clues as to how we were going to get close enough to an elk in this heavily forested area (all but one of us had never even seen the area before) to get a shot with our new open sighted black powder rifles that were limited to about 100 yards.

It was the first of many trips I want to share with you because of the valuable insights we learned together about the elk, about life and relationships, and most importantly, about a relationship with our Creator. Our elk hunting adventures became spiritual retreats for us because of the challenges, difficulties, disappointments, and truths we learned.

From our elk hunting adventures, we learned about listening to God's voice, how to deal with disappointment, teamwork, prayer and divine guidance, temptation, conflict resolution, perseverance, fellowship, and more. These were lessons that were completely unexpected, but we believed God's Spirit revealed them to us as we strived together to harvest this magnificent big game animal in some of the most beautiful, and yet most rugged and inaccessible real estate on God's great earth.

This book also contains fourteen foundational truths that will conquer predators in your spiritual life. You may want to "Think It Through" on your own or in a group setting so you can discuss these truths openly together and learn from one another as our hunting camp did.

My purpose in writing this book along with the "Think It Through," "Appendix of 44 Hunting Tips," and "Gear Packing List" sections is twofold: to help other sportsmen overcome what can seem like insurmountable challenges in becoming successful in hunting the magnificent bull elk, and to equip them to conquer 14 spiritual or personal life challenges that all of us have to face. My hope is that you will come to recognize what a relationship with Christ can accomplish in your life.

I have included many strategies and hunting tips that have worked for us over the past thirty plus years that I believe will help you to become a better elk hunter. One of the greatest lessons though, is the discovery that Jesus

Christ wants to be there for you in every situation you face in life. He wants to turn disappointments into victories, conflicts into growing times, and weaknesses into strengths. He wants us to learn to work together and find success through persistence.

I have formatted this book with two options in mind, you can read each chapter on your own and then consider turning to the "Think It Through" section for a deeper search for personal insights; or read each chapter in preparation for a group setting and discuss the chapter and the "Think It Through" section together. Choosing the second option gives you the added opportunity to share each other's insights about the elk hunting strategies I've addressed in each chapter.

In addition, I have included a copy of my much used and very refined check list of packing gear you'll need on your September "do-it-yourself" elk hunting trip. You will be tempted to bring more gear than what I suggest, but if you are packing up into a high elevation camp like we do, don't bring one more pound than what I have included in the list.

The appendix of hunting strategies is a list I have developed over many years of hunting and research. It's a list I still bring with me on hunting trips and review before I go. In crunch times, you have to be able to think fast and think smart and nobody gets it right all the time, but you can at least do your homework and raise your odds of success. Lastly, go to my website and share your stories of how this book helped you create an adventure, find success in hunting the majestic bull elk or discover God's ultimate plan for your life: **guidetobuglingbulls.com.**

I pray that this book will lead you into a stronger and more purpose-filled life than you ever dreamed possible. Just put on your hunting boots and get ready for an adventurous climb up a mountain to harvest some great bulls and conquer some big life challenges. Go with me back into God's country in search of a magnificent game animal.

1 Disappointment

It was the end of the first day of hunting in our high Colorado elk camp, and what we saw in Ross' face was the epitome of disappointment as we'd never seen it before. Ross refused to talk about it at first, but we slowly dragged it out of him.

Ross is a big guy with a big heart and a lot of emotion. In a future story I'll tell you about a trip where he single-handedly carried a big wall tent almost two miles on a rocky, narrow mountain trail that gained five hundred feet in elevation to our camp! He wasn't just big; he was strong, but with a quiet demeanor. And Ross was a storyteller, with a way of embellishing on every detail to give you a play-by-play dramatic description of what happened. Ross had gone up and over to the other side of the mountain ridge by himself that morning, and there he found a small rockslide just over the edge and down about 100 yards into that new canyon. He was sitting near the top when he spotted some cow elk moving through just below the rockslide, about 100 yards away.

Because he's a very experienced hunter and grew up learning about hunting whitetails from his dad who was a biologist, he thought a bull might be following behind just like a buck would do, so he got his gun up and made sure he was ready. That's when the biggest bull elk he'd ever seen in his life swung its long sweeping antlers between the trees and stepped out into the opening. He kept telling us the antlers were so long they touched the big bull's rump! It was enormous! Ross, who without a doubt has two of the sharpest eyes and is one of the best shots I know, leveled off on the bull's shoulder and squeezed the trigger of his .50 caliber muzzleloader. Instantly, smoke filled the air, and the next thing he knew the bull and cows were gone. Moments later, the sky opened up, and it began to pour down rain.

Ross' adrenalin was pumping, he had to find that bull, but the blood trail was washed away by the unpredictable high Rocky Mountain downpour. He searched and searched and reached down deep inside for the tracking abilities he'd honed over his many years of whitetail archery hunting, but he found nothing. The bull was gone! It had disappeared into the thick forest. Disappointment began to sweep over him as he relived the drama, re-thinking his shot placement and trying to recall how the animal had reacted to the shot. He was sure that everything was right, but the bull was gone. Now he was lying on his cot with his head under the covers, refusing to come out, believing he had just lost the trophy of a lifetime.

The next day was Sunday. Unfortunately, it was raining heavily outside our tent, and Ross' head was still under the covers refusing to come out. We decided this was a good time to head down the mountain and attend morning worship at a small church in a nearby town. As it turned out, that church service for us was like a spring of cold water for a dying man's thirst. We all sat there and just drank in all the words of encouragement and faith after the previous day's disappointment. The songs, the pastor's message, the testimony, the prayer time, it all lifted us up out of our discouragement and gave us, especially Ross, a renewed hope.

That evening, Paul and I decided to go out and hunt just above camp, walking slowly while making cow calls every five minutes or so. Paul also came from a family that loved whitetail hunting. His dad owned a family dairy farm with about 100 cows. Paul, with his brother Randy, worked the farm together with their dad, but they also spent a lot of time learning how to hunt whitetails on their land.

After we became separated, Paul suddenly thought he heard a bull coming to his call, presumably looking for that lone cow he was trying to imitate. Paul knew he had to freeze while the bull made a slow and careful sweep around his hidden position. At just 25 yards, the bull stopped broadside, and Paul nervously made what he thought was a good shot on the five-by-five bull.

Paul is a very self-controlled and happy guy, like his dad, and he can get along with most anybody that he meets. He was strong too, and I have seen him carry some packs on his back that looked ridiculously heavy, but you never heard him whine or complain about it. Normally Paul didn't show his emotions much at all; he usually seemed to focus more on the facts than how the facts made you feel. And he had a way of trying to bring out the best in the people he was around, maybe because he very unselfishly seemed to think the best about them. He also is a good whitetail hunter, and in future stories you'll discover that he had two very sharp eyes and an unusual ability to track wounded animals.

When I met up with him again he was really nervous about where the bull had gone and whether or not he had made a good shot. He pointed me in the direction where he last saw it, and I slowly tried to find tracks or blood. I hadn't gone more than 100 yards when I jumped the bull. All I had was a rear end shot, so I took it hoping to connect with his neck. But the bull disappeared with so much racket that he sounded like a herd of animals crashing through the thick cover. Elk are big and heavy and can make a lot of noise when they are in a hurry. Darkness quickly overcame us so we made our way back to camp, but we were two of the most excited hunters in the world, feeling good about the possibility of recovering the bull the next day.

We all got up early the next morning ready to go look for the bull. We had to climb straight up above camp, and the first 300 yards were really steep and covered with thick, boot-tripping grass. But Paul and I both had some adrenalin running through our veins, pushing us up that hill a little faster. We carried our pack frames, knives, and game bags with us as we slowly pushed our way toward the last sighting of the elk. We all had our eyes on the ground, looking for blood or tracks, and we found just enough to help keep us on the right trail.

One of the guys pushed ahead at a faster pace, hoping to spot the bull, and within about 20 minutes, he spotted the big tan body of the elk on the ground. All of us were relieved and rejoicing, high fives and even hugs were abundant. This five-by-five bull, our first as a hunting team with a muzzleloader, seemed like the trophy of a lifetime to all of us.

We didn't really know what we were doing; we just slowly stalked our way through the forest while cow calling regularly, hoping that a bull that was moving through would hear the call and come to check us out. It was a great feeling of success when we saw that huge animal lying on the ground with his antlers pointing up toward the sky. It felt like the Lord had rewarded us for seeking and putting Him first that Sunday morning, and for seeking His strength to rise up out of the disappointment we had all been feeling with Ross.

On that Monday morning, we boned and packed out the meat, but we weren't giving up on what Ross had started. We were going to make sure that he was going to fully resolve his disappointment and get another opportunity at his bull.

Paul and I had to convince Ross he should go back up to the rockslide so we could help him search the area some more and at least look for signs of that big boy he thought he'd connected with on Saturday. So on Tuesday morning, all three of us slowly headed up the mountain, cow calling frequently on our way through the timber, trying to sound like a small herd of cows that any nearby bull might want to check out. After a few hours, we made it to the top of the ridge and found our way over to the area where he thought he had made the shot. What we discovered was another smaller rockslide that looked very much like the rockslide on which Ross had wounded that trophy bull. It was still, foggy, super quiet and right at noon, so we sat down in the middle of the rocks to have lunch and enjoy the pica as they chirped and scurried about the ground.

We could see enough to know that there was a very deep, thick, timber-filled canyon down below us. Every ten minutes or so, Ross or Paul would give a cow call, and then we'd all listen for even a faint reply from a bull. They had only cow called three times when a bugle sounded from the canyon deep below us. Wow did we get excited, and Ross and I scurried over the rocks to find a place where we could find a shooting lane into the timber. Paul called again and the bull responded immediately, but this time it sounded as if he were a lot closer, covering ground and elevation at a very exciting pace.

Hearing that bull scream at us even though he was still a long way away made my heart jump into a much faster rhythm. I knew Paul's heart was doing the same because some of his cow calls sounded more like a crow than a cow! He was also trying to run a video camera at the same time, and the pictures we looked at later included a lot of rocks, sky, and dizzying movements. I'm not sure how long the whole thing lasted; it seemed like only minutes, but they were very exciting minutes for us three young and adventurous hunters.

A few more calls and the bull came right up to the edge of the timber under the rockslide and stopped 25 yards directly below Ross. Big Ross aimed more carefully than he had ever aimed in his life, held his rifle tightly to his shoulder, and squeezed the trigger of his .50 caliber again. He did not miss, and as we discovered about an hour later, the bull did not go far. Paul and I were insistent that we give the bull an hour before we got on the blood trail, so we broke for lunch while listening to Ross re-tell the story over and over in a very excited and impatient voice. He really wanted to go look for the elk right away, but we were just beginning to learn that a big animal like this takes time to expire. We were also discovering that our muzzleloaders did not have the same killing power as a high powered rifle.

Finally we got on the trail, and it was immediately evident that the bull was hit well. We found a good blood trail and after only about 70 yards, an ecstatic Ross had a nice five-by-five bull to tag. There was no question in our minds that the main reason he was successful was because he did not allow his disappointment to keep him from trying again. We sat there by the animal thinking about all that had just happened, over-whelmed with how the Lord had helped us get from "the agony of defeat" to "the thrill of victory." It was a lesson I would never forget about how to deal with disappointment.

See "Think It Through"– page 78

2 TEAMWORK

One of the most memorable early elk hunts I've been on was our second muzzleloader hunt in 1996 to Colorado. We found ourselves without any elk in camp and only one and a half days left to hunt. Mark and I made our way down a trail that followed a small rapid creek through some dark timber. The trail met an old logging road that led us back to our camp just as darkness covered us. To our left was a steep southeast facing aspen and evergreen mixed ridge that held some large meadows down in the lower elevations. We thought the elk might move from their bedding down to feed in those meadows at night. We had heard a bull moving in front of us up on that ridge as we neared the creek, but now—suddenly—the bull let out a scream not more than 300 yards away. The high pitched and angry sounding roar made the hair on the back of my neck stand on end. The thought of cow calling hit my mind, just to see how he would react, but I immediately rejected that because I was intimidated by the bull's closeness and his loud scream in the darkness!

We stood there in the dark listening to the bull bugle over and over while mentally following his course along the ridge. Mark is Paul's oldest brother, and he is a very physically fit kind of guy who would do almost anything for anybody. As a hunter, Mark may be known more for his speed and endurance than for how many animals he has harvested. In a future story you'll read how he wounded two different bulls in the same week before he finally harvested a bull on one of our final days. In between, we covered a lot of ground fast! Generally, Mark shows his emotions more than Paul or their brother Randy, yet he is a guy that can take a lot of pain without complaining.

Our season was almost over so we felt excited about the possibility of cutting this big boy off the next morning, if he'd follow the same general trail back up to his bed. When we arrived at camp an hour later, Paul had a story that seemed to connect with ours. He'd been hunting alone and on the opposite side of the creek we came down when he got into a herd of cows and a big screaming bull that he just couldn't get close enough to see. From the details of his exciting story, Mark and I felt confident that it was the same bull he and I had encountered. Paul had been cow calling and stalking but the bull kept moving and pushing his cows ahead of him. Most elk hunters know that a herd bull is one of the toughest elk to harvest because of all the eyes and ears of the herd he has with him, and the tendency to keep his cows moving constantly when they think a competing bull is in the area.

Paul always became really intense when he got close to a bull, and it seemed like his big eyes were almost glowing with excitement in the dark. You need to know that he's a very no-nonsense, "use your head" kind of guy; but he also has a very spiritual side to him and a unique sensitivity to God. But that night I saw a part of him that I had never encountered before. He told us that as he ran out of light and time pursuing the bull, he believed he heard God speak to his heart and say, "Your team will get this bull, but you have to work together." Wow, I couldn't believe this was happening, except for the fact we were discovering new spiritual insights from the Lord every time we came to what was becoming a sacred mountain. Plus, what Mark and I had just experienced as we heard the bull moving through gave us plenty of evidence and hope that we could be successful in getting the bull.

The next morning we were up early in anticipation of harvesting this bull and together the six of us set out into the dark toward that steep ridge we eventually nicknamed, "Bull Hill." We had a plan, but before we could even get to the creek an hour later, we heard the bull screaming and moving up toward the ridge we'd heard him on the night before. We had to make a little adjustment to our plan because the bull was up earlier and moving faster than we had anticipated, so we decided that the guys with the best climbing legs would head up together then split off at different intervals to try to cut him off.

My idea was that he'd come back on about the same elevation Mark and I had heard him go on the night before, so I opted to take the lower level. The hill was so steep and we were moving so quickly that I thought I'd die trying to keep up with Mark and Dan as they led the way! I can tell you from personal experience that anyone who wants to hunt elk in the rugged Rocky Mountains had better come physically prepared for some challenging workouts.

Dan is a smaller, imaginative, and very comical kind of guy that we nicknamed, "Rambo." The reason he earned that title goes back to our very first elk hunting trip with "smoke poles" in 1993. Dan wore this Rambo-like scarf around his head and light shoes on his feet and he seemed to nearly run through the mountains in search of a big bull. I remember the first day of that hunt when Dan was trying to bugle in a bull down below me. I could hear him bugle and I could hear a bull bugle, but the bull wasn't moving toward Dan, it was moving away from him. As I followed his bugles with my ears, the bull crossed the creek and climbed a very steep ridge in thick timber not more than 250 yards below where I was sitting. Then I could hear him bugling as he made his way along the side of the ridge and head up into higher country. I later followed his tracks up that steep mountain side and spent my first afternoon investigating what we later nicknamed, "Bull Hill."

On one particular day, Mark and Dan were hunting together and I think they almost literally ran over some elk! It almost seemed like the elk were not able to stay ahead of those two "Rambo's!" Actually, they did almost have an opportunity to get a shot at a bull, but in the thick cover they couldn't get a clear shot even though they were very close. But on their way around the whole canyon, they got a bit lost and wandered off onto the wrong side of the canyon, the backside of which was a virtually vertical rocky cliff! They did somehow get back to camp, but not until just before midnight. Even though as a team our knowledge about how to hunt elk was in its immature stages, our level of endurance and ability to find our way through unfamiliar country was not.

So, back on "Bull Hill," I found the position where I wanted to try to cut off this hot bull, and it didn't take long before I heard him coming, screaming, and letting the world know that he was the boss. It's an adrenalin rush that I've never experienced with any other kind of hunt. At first he was slightly below me, but he was coming in my general direction through an aspen area that was fairly open. Back then I didn't even own a bugle, so the plan was very simple: just wait and try to get in front of him. Suddenly, he was moving to a higher elevation, so I adjusted several times and moved higher while also trying to stay hidden behind stumps and brush in what was now a sparse mix of pines and aspen.

It wasn't long before he was just on the other side of some really thick cover he was using to help hide his movements, only about 60 yards away. On public land like this, the bulls don't come out into the open until after dark very often. Then, he appeared above me maybe 70 yards up and let out another scream that seemed to penetrate through my body and my nerves. He was big, beautiful, and magnificent as he stood for just a moment to lay his head back and bugle and then began walking again, making his way through a little opening that provided me with a nice broadside shot. His sweeping antlers looked huge, but I knew I had to focus on the chest area and squeeze the trigger as he was walking. I carefully leveled the front sight right behind his front shoulder and pulled the trigger, the gun roared and the air turned blue. I watched the big guy merely flinch, as if nothing more than a bug had just bit him! I was expecting that 350 grain bullet to have a bit more of an effect!

Then he turned downhill and began to walk right toward me! I froze, out of fear for one thing, not knowing what he had in mind. When I realized I was holding an empty gun, I nervously fumbled through my pockets looking for a reload but couldn't seem to find one. He walked no more than 15 yards from me, and I can still clearly remember seeing the .50 caliber hole in his side, right in the middle of his body. I was surprised by the lack of blood coming from the bullet hole in his side. I expected it to be pouring out; instead there was only a small red stain under it. I was concerned at the lack of blood flowing from the wound, but I remember having a feeling of exhilaration and success and in my mind as I mentally said to the bull, "You're mine!"

After he passed by me, I quickly found a reload and concentrated on getting every grain down the barrel (in Colorado pelletized powder is not allowed), but when I looked up, the big bull was gone. At that moment it seemed like our team effort had really worked, just as Paul had predicted the night before.

I excitedly looked for the bull's trail, but there was very little blood and not much for tracks in the dry hard ground. All the guys eventually came, and we went to work tracking the wounded animal together. The trail led us over a very small creek and up a very steep game trail. After we had climbed up the 30 foot incline, we discovered a very fresh bed right at the top edge, but the bull was gone. He probably had seen us trailing him, then busted for higher, safer ground. After that, the blood trail disappeared.

It's a real emotional roller-coaster ride when your first trophy bull vanishes into thin air with a huge hole in his side! We spent nearly the rest of the day searching for but not finding him, and all of us were becoming so disappointed that we began to question Paul's prediction, my shot, and how things were really going to work out! In my mind I kept seeing that hole in the bull's side as he walked right past me. It just did not seem possible that he could make it this far or that such a big animal could just disappear into the forest.

The next morning, after an unbelievable search I'll tell you about in our next chapter on "Guidance," we found the big six-by-five bull the Lord had promised us. According to the GPS, he was lying half a mile from where I'd shot him. It's an unbelievable story that leaves me in awe every time I think about it. You will read what Paul Harvey would have called "The rest of the story," and it is proof again that teamwork really pays big dividends.

See "Think It Through" – page 79

3 GUIDANCE

I had just pulled the trigger on the biggest bull of my elk-hunting career to date, after a fantastic team effort put me in the right place at the right time with a muzzleloader. The problem was that the blood trail was so hard to find that it took all five of us to stay on it. The bull had walked parallel to the ridge I shot him on for several hundred yards then climbed a steep 30 foot creek edge into some very thick cover. He then laid down right on the top edge where he could look down and watch his back trail. I've since discovered that a wounded bull elk will do this often.

On one trip years later while I was trailing a bull I had hit with an arrow on some light snow, I discovered that he would stand on ledges above and watch for me to come, and then he would take off and move to his next lookout. That bull must have done that a half a dozen times at least. Of course, we were just beginning to learn about elk behaviors on this second trip, so we discovered it the hard way, after we had jumped him and lost the blood trail all together! It was a hard lesson that taught us to wait at least an hour before trailing a big bull hit by a muzzleloader bullet, although the newer copper clad bullets are far better today.

We spent the rest of the morning and early afternoon combing the side of the ridge in the hope of finding the six-by-five bull. But we came up short and finally gave up, even though I knew I had a good shot through the big animal's ribs. I had even seen the hole at 15 yards, but maybe it was just an inch or two too far back and into the liver area. That would give the bull a little more time to get farther away in this vast wilderness area with his long legs and strong body.

I just couldn't give the search up because I knew I had hit him hard; plus, I couldn't let go of Paul's words the night before when he told us he believed God had told him we would get the bull if we worked together as a team. The problem was we were packing up to leave by noon, so the pressure to find him was enormous. Ross has always been considered one of the best trackers in our group, so I asked him to go with me and help me give it one last effort. We worked our way up the deep creek bottom where we had ended our search the day before. We were about a quarter mile below where I had wounded the elk, but rather than climbing the steep ridge on the other side of the creek (because at that time we believed that a mortally wounded elk would not go up a steep incline) we stayed alongside the stream. We were about to discover that our theory about what a wounded bull would do was very wrong. We were greatly underestimating the strength and endurance of this animal.

We came across some day-old tracks that crossed the creek and found what looked like blood, but it was questionable. We crossed the creek and searched for awhile, but could not find any more tracks or blood. Then we made the mistake of going back and heading up the creek again. Later we split up so we could cover more ground.

After searching for awhile we became separated, and I decided to cross back over the creek on my left. It was a move that went against my best judgment at the time, but nothing else was working so why not move up the steeper ridge and see what happens! In this big, heavily forested country, it's almost impossible to know where to start searching, but Ross had suggested I try to look in some thicker bedding areas. So, against my belief that a mortally wounded elk would not walk uphill, I began climbing slowly up into the thicker areas while also moving back toward the trail we had come in on.

I recall feeling overwhelmed by the immense area that I needed to search; so as I wandered along, I started to quietly pray, talking to the God who had created this vast country and the animals that lived in it, asking for his guidance. At one point, I was so desperate I prayed out loud in frustration, "Lord, which way should I go?" You may have prayed a similar prayer during a crisis in your life. It was one of those times when you throw your hands up in the air while feeling totally overwhelmed by the situation and difficulty of the moment.

This may sound presumptuous, but I really sensed in my heart that God said to me, "Go where you believe you should go." I wasn't totally sure where that was, but I moved up even higher in elevation until I recognized a wallow in the heavy timber. I remembered crossing it three years earlier as we brought Ross' bull down from the rockslide area which I wrote about in the first chapter. By this time I believed I didn't have more than maybe a few hundred yards to go before I needed to head back down to the creek and give up the hunt, the search would be over and the trophy would be lost.

I slowly walked another 100 yards, then suddenly felt disappointment hit me like a canon ball to my stomach as I verbalized my next thought, "I have to give up." It was one of those moments when disappointment overwhelms you as you have to face the fact that you've done all you could do, but you've come up short and failure is staring you squarely in the face. I gave up and verbalized the thoughts that, "It's out of my hands. I've done all I can do. It's over. I've got to leave this in God's hands." At that exact moment, a late morning switch of the thermal wind currents caught my attention.

It was little more than a slight movement of air, but it carried with it something every elk hunter would die for in a moment like this: the strong, pungent smell of a rutting bull elk. It was so strong I decided to take one more chance and try to follow it with my nose uphill to the best of my scenting abilities. I still remember following my nose as it led me up that hill like a dog after a bird. I really didn't have anything to lose by trying. The strong odor led me up for what I thought was over 100 yards. The smell got stronger, so I continued moving up until my eye caught something that looked out of place. A sense of excitement grew in me as I stared at it wondering if it was possible that this was part of an antler tip.

I cautiously moved up with my gun ready and in a matter of seconds I could tell that it was an antler that I was seeing, a big antler, and it was attached to a big tan colored body! I remember saying to myself over and over again, "I can't believe I found it! I can't believe it!" My sense of unbelief was so strong that my next thought was, "Is this really the same bull I wounded?" It wasn't a very rational thought because we hadn't seen any other hunters in the area, but it does illustrate my state of mind at the time and my unbelief that he could have climbed this high with a mortal wound. I quickly confirmed by the size and shape of the antlers and the placement of the bullet hole that it was my elk, and what a party I had! I let out a victory cry and shot my gun off to celebrate and to alert Ross. I was so pumped that I re-loaded and shot again! What I didn't know was that Ross was too far away to hear the shots and had already given up and left.

I called Mark and Paul on the two-way radio and announced our search had been a success, and then I gave them my approximate location. They said they were up on top of the mountain on a rock pile viewing the beautiful mountains and asking the Lord for His guidance for Ross and me. I'm not sure why they went to the top of the mountain, or what they were expecting to find way up there. I can only assume that maybe Mark was aggressively leading the way and Paul couldn't slow him or stop him, but I could be wrong.

I knew I needed everybody to help in boning and packing out the big animal as quickly as possible, so I field-dressed him, confirmed that the meat was still good, then marked the area with plastic orange-colored marking tape and left a clear trail with it all the way down to the creek. I wasn't about to lose this trophy again, so I used a lot of tape! But I always pull the tape and take it with me on the way out. Then I hiked down to the logging road and flew back to camp on the four-wheeler. There wasn't a man in our group who wasn't astounded by the improbability of finding that bull. We all knew that it was nothing less than the divine guidance of God's Spirit in answer to some intense prayers by a team of some desperate hunters.

See "Think It Through" – page 80

4 CONFLICTS

It was a dark and rainy night and Paul and I were headed back to camp after a long day of elk hunting. Normally, we leave camp in the dark of morning and don't return until an hour or more after dark at night. We try to be in the best elk areas as the sun is rising or setting and elk movement is at its peak, so we have to find our way in the dark a lot. It can be very challenging to do that in this big country, so I've found that a good GPS unit combined with a compass can make the trip much safer, easier, and more productive. Because it was so wet that night, we decided to discharge our muzzleloaders on the trail instead of waiting until we got back to camp. That proved to be a big mistake.

After we arrived at camp more than a half hour later, we found that everyone else was back except Dan. Supper was ready, so we dug in while sharing stories about our day of hunting. Much later, Dan finally made it back to camp looking like he'd had a pretty rough day. We had made a rule that if someone was in trouble they should fire off their gun two or three times to signal for help; so, when Dan, who had been hunting below our route back to camp, heard our shots, he surmised that someone was in trouble and needed help. He'd set out walking up hill through the dark, wet, and thick forest in a direct line toward the shots. It was really a miserable route for him. When he finally made it to the trail, no one was there, so he decided to turn toward camp to try to find out if someone was missing and in trouble.

When he questioned us, we regretfully admitted that we had fired our guns on the trail instead of waiting until we got back to camp without considering that someone might hear us and think we were in trouble. He was not happy with what we'd done, and it didn't take long for Paul and me to figure that out. We'd broken the rule, and he had paid a miserable price for it. He was very upset with us, and he articulated it to us in a way that clearly communicated his feelings about the situation.

What should we do next? None of us seemed to know. Paul and I both felt terrible about it. I had never seen Dan get so upset. All of us clammed up for a while, unsure of what to do or how to diffuse the bomb we all knew was lying on the table. Something had to be done. There was no way any of us wanted this mistake to ruin our trip. I'm not sure what everyone else tried to do; I believe that at least one of the guys tried to say something to Dan to help diffuse the conflict, but I finally decided that I should apologize regardless of what anyone else did. I waited until all our emotions calmed down a little, then went to Dan and personally apologized for my inconsiderate actions. Dan was receptive and forgiving, and it didn't take long at all before our fellowship was restored and things were back to normal for all of us.

For me, the whole episode brought back bad memories of a much earlier elk hunt I'd been on with a totally different group of guys. We were rifle hunting for elk, but one person in our group decided he was only interested in buying a deer tag, which sold for a much lower price, even though he planned on helping us get some elk with his rifle. It was obviously illegal, and I for one wanted nothing to do with any illegal hunting practices. Sometimes we all make unintentional mistakes. We may even break the law because of a mistake in judgment, like the time we ignorantly cut off the body parts that confirmed the sex of the animal one of us had harvested! But this was a very intentional and premeditated plan to violate the law.

The whole thing blew up a few days later after I voiced my disapproval and our group split up. Two of the guys left and went to hunt on their own. We did end up getting one big 6x6 bull the legal way. But when we finally got back to Wisconsin, there was another explosive confrontation among three of us that I thought would end in a fistfight. The person who was the angriest and most out of control, however, was the same person who was guilty of the hunting violation! How the person who had planned the illegal hunt from the beginning could be the angriest was confusing to me. I can forgive anyone who is willing to take responsibility for their mistakes, but that wasn't happening in this situation.

Thankfully, a day or two later he came to my home to take responsibility for his actions and personally apologized to me. It resolved things between us, but his relationship with the third person remained distant for years afterward. The whole thing caused me to make a decision that I wouldn't go on another hunting trip for some time, and if I ever did go again, I'd have to be absolutely certain about whom I was going with and what their intentions were. In a way, I guess it was my own fault that I hadn't understood everyone's plans before we left Wisconsin. There weren't any planning meetings to air everyone's ideas and plans like we always do now.

Thankfully, Dan and this group of elk hunters were committed to communicating personal plans and goals before we left and equally committed to working through our differences during our trip. The whole thing became a great lesson to me on the importance of taking personal responsibility for our own actions to resolve and prevent conflict.

See "Think It Through" – page 81

5 PERSEVERANCE

It didn't take more than seconds for the bull to answer my bugle, and another exciting encounter with a majestic elk was in the works for Joe, Paul, and me. We were moving closer to the bull because I was learning that it doesn't pay to just sit there hoping the bull is going to come to you. Occasionally, that will happen, but most of the time I have found that it is more productive to move in closer and challenge the big boy on his own turf. I prefer to get within 100 yards before I bugle again, but it all depends on the mood of the animal. The caller has to try to read the bull's mood before responding, so it's an imperfect and risky science to say the least.

On this particular late morning the bull was located below us, which is what I prefer depending of course on the wind currents. As we attempted a confrontation he just kept moving away and we couldn't keep up with him, and soon we were simply outdistanced. We took a break at noon, had some lunch, and laid in the sun as we caught up on some sleep. We had positioned ourselves in the back of a drainage bowl at about the middle point in elevation between our trail in and the top. Our plan now was to wait until after 2:30 p.m. or so and then begin calling and locating elk as they move again in the afternoon hours toward their feeding areas. I bugled again and had a quick response that was a long way off, so we decided to wait a little longer. The next time I bugled we had a response from directly above us, and this was perfect! Some more bugling revealed he was moving down, but then he stopped, turned around, and headed back up the mountain returning bugles until we could barely hear him anymore.

We had moved our position by now to intercept the bull, but I really thought it was all over because he seemed to be headed back up and over the mountain at a pace that would kill the average man. Paul, however, had a very different idea. Thinking we were staying with him, Paul had moved up the hill and was trying to catch up to and confront the bull. Though the process was slow, he gained a great deal of elevation and found himself in the middle of a small herd that was stopping quite frequently. He would cow call to soothe the herd, and then bugle to locate and fire up the bull. He just kept stalking and moving up, willing to pay whatever price he had to physically to get a chance at the herd bull.

Meanwhile, Joe and I had a bull come down the mountain and cross over the main creek next to us. He was bugling back at us, so we kept up the pursuit until he finally quit answering and left us stranded. At about that same time we heard Paul's muzzleloader fire way up high above us. We couldn't believe it. Had he really stayed with that fast moving bull way up there and gotten a shot?

We learned when we met him later that he had patiently and persistently stayed with the herd, even refusing to take a shot at some smaller rag horns so that he could get a chance at the bigger bull. It was thick timber on a northern exposure that both helped and hindered because while it camouflaged his movements, it also concealed the bull. Finally, he knew his opportunity had come when he heard the bull raking a tree with its antlers. It's a scraping sound that you can hear from even 50 yards away. He knew that this was his opportunity to quickly but carefully move in, knowing the bull was preoccupied. He got within 15 yards when he finally spotted the bull through a small opening. He slowly raised his rifle, aimed behind the front shoulder, and gently squeezed the trigger. The forest filled with blue smoke, and Paul knew his persistence had finally paid off.

The next day there were all kinds of complaints about having to walk so far and climb so high to retrieve the animal. But when we finally got there, the prize of persistence—a nice six-by-six—was lying on the ground to greet us.

That message has been preached to me again and again in elk hunting. Somewhere along the way I picked up the adage that you can't give up too easily. You have to prepare for the hunt, get in good physical shape, hunt hard, and plan on not getting your elk until the final hours of the last day. If you're just starting to hunt elk, plan on having to pay your dues and earn your right to harvest one of these trophies. I'm kind of a fan of Jim Zumbo who wrote in one of his many books on elk hunting (I've read them all), "You can shoot an elk from anyplace except the inside of your tent." What I think he meant was, "Keep going, regardless of the weather or hard challenges, until the last minutes of the last day have passed!

In 2005, that message was again relayed to me as I was awakened by an elk bugle on the morning we were going to pack up and leave camp. My son, David, was the only one still holding a tag, and he was asleep! I lay in my sack listening as light was just beginning to overcome the darkness. We had decided to sleep in that morning because we'd worked so hard all that week.

As I listened to the bugle, I really thought that it was a practical joke by the other two in a separate tent. I whispered, "Is that you guys?" but I heard no response. They told me later they thought maybe we were the ones trying to play a trick on them so they stayed in their sacks! I heard the bull bugle again, and it was clear he was coming closer! In fact, I jumped out of the tent and immediately looked for the gun, but then it hit me, "I don't even have a tag! What am I going to do?" Party hunting is not allowed in Colorado.

Meanwhile, back in his sack still out cold, David, who was worn out from our week of hunting, refused to get up and slept through the whole incident. As I stood there in the twilight knowing that there was nothing I could do, I decided that bull was sent to give us a message. He was either telling us, "Don't sleep in again!", or he was saying, "See you next time!" Either way it was a message about perseverance.

See "Think It Through" – page 82

6 TEMPTATIONS

It really is a rush to fool a big aggressive animal like a bull elk and bring him in so close that even a bow hunter can get a shot in thick cover. Whether the shooter gets the animal or not, as the caller you get a very exhilarating feeling knowing the animal was virtually right in the palm of your hand—right where you wanted him. And he had no clue just how much danger he was in.

I have no doubt that on a spiritual level that is what Satan feels when he draws us into his traps: a sense that he has us in the palm of his hand, a sense of having power over us because of our weaknesses or natural carnal temptations.

I remember one morning when we were calling back and forth with several bugling bulls that I just couldn't get in close enough for a shot at. Randy had harvested a bull the day before, so our whole group was together and hunting on our way to retrieve the downed animal. We were on top of a heavily-timbered mountain ridge straight up above camp that had a long stretch of really large dead falls. These were huge dry logs that made getting through the area a real struggle. There was also a lot of thick new growth on the topside, and we were working the bulls that were coming up the ridge and moving toward the higher ground to their bedding spot in front of us. It seemed like they were coming straight up through the downed timber toward us, but they were actually angling up the ridge, moving far enough ahead of us that we were unable to get a look at even one of them.

One strategy for this situation is to have a hunter move way ahead in a silent stalk, watching the wind and attempting to make a move on the bull while the caller keeps the bull bugling. This way the bull is constantly giving away his location to a hunter so he can be pursued with a silent stalk.

This was my plan on that day, so I sent Joe out ahead because he is very athletic and he was archery hunting, so he was dressed in total camouflage. He had the best legs of any of us so I figured that if anybody could get ahead of the herd, it was Joe. He moved as quickly and silently as he could and even succeeded in getting ahead of the herd. He had one opportunity to take a shot at the big herd bull, but the animal moved through the shooting lane too quickly for Joe to feel comfortable letting the arrow go. An experienced archery hunter like Joe knows he must avoid just wounding the animal, even if it means not taking a shot.

By this time, as far as the rest of us could tell, the herd was gone. They had just moved too quickly, especially for the thick cover we were in. But suddenly, we heard another bull coming up the other side of the ridge in front of us, moving toward a flat area on the top of the ridge not more than 250 yards away. He was moving very quickly and his return calls to our bugle told us he was crossing through the top and dropping down toward the canyon on our left side without any intentions of stopping. He bugled back several times, revealing his location, but just kept moving. Without hesitation we made a very fast-paced and exciting move to where he had crossed in front of us, and I gave a quick bugle. Immediately he stopped and bugled back from down below, indicating to me that he might turn around and come back for a challenge. But we needed to set up and bugle back very quickly. We ran through the timber toward the edge the bull had dropped over, quickly set up, and got ready for a possible opportunity.

This was Rodney's first time hunting with us, and I think he was a little unsure of what to do because things were happening so fast. Rodney is another great whitetail deer hunter with both rifle and bow, but elk hunting requires some very different strategies than ordinary stand hunting for deer. Rodney is the kind of guy who has the patience of Job. As a top notch mechanic, he has won awards from General Motors for his ability to think through and solve difficult problems. He can sit in a stand in the freezing cold weather of November in Wisconsin and think nothing of staying there all day.

I remember grabbing Rodney by the shoulders and excitedly directed him to move down toward the bull at the edge of where it had dropped below us. I could tell that Rodney's whitetail instincts—wanting to move slowly and quietly—were kicking into gear and slowing him down. I'm not sure what he thought of what I was making him do, but the look in his eye was certainly one that seemed to be saying, "You're crazy!" I made sure he got at least 50 yards ahead of me before I called again. David and Joe also set up, and I think I even backed up a little to create some more distance between us and to find a good place to disappear into the cover.

I bugled again, and instantly this hot bull was on his way back up that steep ridge, coming right for us, and moving unnervingly fast. Again, I had the sense that this bull was in the proverbial palm of my hand and was about to fall into my trap. It did not even take 60 seconds, and we could hear him coming up the steep ridge fast with brush cracking and stones rolling down the mountain behind him.

There's just nothing like the experience of having a 600- to 900-pound bull with red eyes, flared nostrils, ears up, and antlers tipped back, on the move and looking for a fight with you! I can imagine that having a bear running toward you would probably surpass the intensity we were experiencing, but I've never hunted for bear. Moments later, Rodney's gun filled the air with smoke, followed by the sounds of a mortally wounded elk running back down the steep ridge making even more racket then he made coming up. Wow, does it ever get your heart pumping!

A few minutes later, Rodney made his way back to me and he seemed dazed with how quickly it had all happened. As the caller, I get at least as excited as the shooter, and I think the shooters even get a little perturbed with all my questions about what happened because I rarely get to see the animal. For all of us, it was that "thrill of victory" feeling that sports announcers talk about.

It wasn't long before we were over the edge, and Rodney was taking a second shot to finish off the animal. A bull hit even in the lungs will often take at least half an hour to expire, so it's best to just be patient, sit down and wait an hour. Soon we were all sitting next to Rodney's nice five-by-five bull, his first muzzleloader elk. We had lured the big animal in to Rodney's sights. He'd come right to where we wanted him because he fell for our deceiving trap.

Just a few days after that successful hunt, my son David, (who was archery hunting on a youth tag), Joe, and I were moving up toward a saddle between two peaks on another heavily-timbered ridge. Suddenly a bull answered our bugle. We scrambled forward about 100 yards as quickly as we could and bugled again. The bull once again returned our call, so we waited for about ten minutes to see if he would come to us. But the next time the bull bugled he was much farther away, so we quickly moved again directly toward him, gaining in elevation and heart rate as we did so. This was one of our last days to hunt in the nine-day season, and we had hunted every day. Plus we had carried two bulls back to our camp on our backs, so I for one was getting physically worn out. We hunt on public land without the help of horses or four-wheelers, so it is very challenging physically.

We kept up the pursuit of this bull until he finally slowed his retreat, allowing us to get within about 100 yards of him. Sometimes an elk will move downwind of the caller and try to get a whiff of your scent just to be sure it's really another bull challenging him and not some sneaky humans. So, we had David stalk parallel with us about 50 yards downwind as we moved quickly toward him. What happened next is something bow hunters dream about. The bull had gotten so worked up that he stopped to rake a tree with his antlers, and this gave us the opportunity to get in very close for a shot.

When I finally got a look at the bull, he was standing with his face toward me. The tree he was taking his aggression out on was getting a serious beating. Joe was in front of me and less than 20 yards from the bull, so I maintained my position and continued bugling. I grabbed a tree branch and started to scrape my own tree to imitate what the bull was doing. Now that he was all worked up, I wanted him to believe that the aggressor he was being challenged by was just as aggressive. I was breaking branches and making as much noise as I could, cutting my hand in the process. I was hoping the bull would move toward me or at least allow Joe to maneuver through the thick cover and get a shot while the bull was destroying the tree. Wow, was it ever exciting to have this wild animal so deceived about who we were and what our intentions were!

The bull finally decided to come my way for a fight, which was supposed to give Joe a perfect broadside shot. I could almost taste the tenderloins as I watched the drama unfold before me. But what happened next was a bow hunter's worst nightmare as the bull came directly toward Joe, coming within about seven yards of him but offering no shot at all. Suddenly, the bull either saw him or smelled him and spun around, realizing he'd been deceived and drawn into a trap. Joe was at full draw, but his only shot was a quick release at the bull's lungs as it turned to run away from him. The good news is he did not wound the elk superficially; the bad news is we had gotten so close, we had drawn him into the proverbial palm of our hands, but he escaped our ambush and disappeared into the thick forest unharmed. We were left standing with empty hands and disappointed hearts.

Joe is not an emotional guy; he's more of a quiet, deep thinker. He's a business major helping to run a successful family lumber business. Though his moves and decisions are always rational and intentional, that close encounter had a deep, emotional impact on him. It left him so disappointed and feeling so overwhelmed by the flood of frustrating feelings that rushed over him that he just disappeared for a while, needing to be alone. There is such a rush when you finally succeed in harvesting a majestic animal in this overwhelmingly big and steep country! But there's also a huge wave of disappointment and frustration when in the final seconds of a heart-throbbing hunt something suddenly goes wrong and the trophy disappears, somehow winning his own battle with temptation.

See "Think It Through" – page 84

7 FELLOWSHIP

Bob, Ross and I had just sat down to take a little lunch break after having a bull silently come to our bugle, bust from the cover, and run back down through the dense forest. Suddenly I heard an excited voice on my walkie-talkie calling my name, "Hey, PC! You'll never guess where we are and what just happened!" Actually, we did have a clue because we'd heard the faint echo of a gunshot in the next canyon, the same canyon that we told the three musketeers on my radio to stay out of because it was so far from camp!

It had been a tough hunting year physically because when we arrived at our trailhead off the highway with our full truckload of gear and four wheelers, we were greeted by an unfamiliar sign and closed gate. A local four wheel drive club had decided to no longer maintain a remote trail that led up to our camp, and the DNR wanted beavers and moose to inhabit the lower area, so foot travel was now the only permitted method for getting up the rocky four-wheel drive road. We had to haul our gear on our backs, including a large wall tent, up the steep, rutted trail. It seemed like two miles to the camp! It was beyond what any of us had ever had to endure physically, including past hunts when we carried out two bull elk on a pack frame from a canyon two drainages away from our truck.

The voice on the radio continued, "Guess what mountain peak we're looking at?" Of course it was the peak on the opposite side of the next canyon. Then they laughed and announced that Chad had just harvested his first bull elk. "We need some help to bone it out and bring it down to the meadow." When I relayed that message to the two guys who were with me, their first response was not a happy one. I heard something like, "We told those guys not to shoot an elk over there." Thinking back, it sounds kind of funny now, but at the time we were all so fatigued by the pack in that it was anything but funny.

I'll have to admit I wasn't very happy about the work that was lying in front of us either. In spite of all that, I told the happy trio in the next canyon that I'd be there as soon as I could; so, down I went into the back of the drainage, making my way through some of the thickest and wettest elk country you could imagine. I knew basically where I needed to go, plus I always carry my GPS with me. I climbed up the ridge on the other side and crossed up and over the next ridge to where I found the giddy trio in the high country of Colorado.

Their story went something like this: "We were just out for a walk and decided to go up and over to see what was on the other side of the ridge. Then, after we bugled, several bulls started bugling back at us, so we decided we should keep on calling just to see what would happen. One particular bull walked just below us and had a bugle that sounded more like a growl, as if his throat were really sore or his bugle was worn out. But we didn't go down after him because we knew that would be too far away! But this other bull kept calling from way down in the canyon. We switched to cow calling in between the bugling and he came right in. What else could we do but shoot? Joe even had a broad side shot with the bow at 40 yards or so, but he decided to let Chad take the higher percentage shot with the muzzleloader. We really didn't come over here to kill an elk!" Giggling followed that and a few slaps on the back.

I lightened up, congratulated Chad, and then inquired about what their plan was for getting the big beast off the mountain. Paul had a plan. We could cut two long poles about six feet in length, lash two-foot cross members between with some light rope, lay the quarters on top, and simply drag the meat down the mountain through the thick forest! He said something about what he'd seen the Native Americans do in some old western television show.

Everybody wanted to avoid having to re-climb back up to the elk with pack frames the next day and there weren't any other great ideas; so, together we went to work cutting up the elk, cutting poles with our knives, and lashing our primitive carriers together with some nylon string somebody had in his pack.

After a few hours, we were ready to head up to the top of the ridge and then over and down through the thick timber to the meadow far below. The only problem was our carriers refused to jump over all the logs that lay in our path, or they'd slide sideways downhill and bump into trees. It didn't take long to figure out that "Plan A" was not working.

We had only two other ideas: leave the meat and come all the way back up with pack frames later, or pick up the carriers and start carrying them down hill. We chose the latter and began our decent. It was a long way to the bottom, climbing over big dead falls, arms straining, forearms burning, shoulders aching. By the time we got to the meadow below, we were all worn out and our backs were aching, but we made it. Now we could walk the four miles back to camp, get our pack frames and our two other partners, and come back for the meat later.

It was a physically difficult journey for all of us, but we made it together. By working as a team of men with a united goal, we overcame the difficulty we were faced with and were now celebrating the success we had achieved together. We hid the meat and came back later to bone the quarters. After we returned, we placed the meat in heavy game bags, put the bags in plastic bags, strapped it to our frames, and carried it down to our camp. Then we took the game bags of meat out of the plastic bags and hung it in a tree to cool overnight.

The next day we could drop it in the creek in sealed plastic bags to stay cool and protect it from the flies. In all the years we've taken care of our meat this way, we've never lost a pound to spoiling. The key is getting it cooled down quickly and adequately, and then the water in the mountain stream is cool enough to maintain a preserving temperature.

We threw those primitive carriers under a big pine tree at the edge of the meadow because they had served their purpose, and we were finished with them. But in a sense, they became icons or reminders of the victory of the hunt and the pain we endured to overcome the challenge of getting the harvest out. Today they are still there, and since that day many years ago I have passed them on several occasions. Each time I get a warm feeling as they remind me of the fellowship that developed that day.

I haven't forgotten how much work it was and how exhausted we were, but what stands out the most is how our fellowship held together under pressure and endured the trial. I have even brought my son David past those rotting pieces of wood and found myself unable to resist stopping to tell him the story of what we accomplished together. The fruit of good fellowship is worth sharing with every new generation.

See "Think It Through" – page 85

8 HEALING

Paul's six-by-six bull was on the ground, but it was about five miles from camp and well over 500 feet up in elevation. It was going to take a big effort from our whole hunting party to bring it down. It had already been a tough hunt because the National Forest Service had closed the gate on our trail, forcing us unexpectedly to pack all our equipment up to our campsite.

One of our hunting partners, Ross, who is a big man weighing about 290, had pushed himself to the limit carrying up the heaviest parts of our gear, and now his lower back was really starting to bother him. He wasn't sure he could make the trek at all, but he was willing to try.

The first leg of our journey was an old, rocky, two-mile logging road that meandered through the fir trees and ended after crossing a small white-water creek. The second leg ran upstream along the edge of the creek on a trail of logs, mud, weeds, and rocks. And with several creek crossings things get really interesting on the way back when you have a heavy pack on your back and legs that are getting weak after a long hard hike.

We were just over halfway on the first leg of our trip when Ross suddenly fell down on the side of the road. His back had taken all it could, and poor Ross was helplessly lying in the dirt unable to get up or even move. There was no way he was ever going to even finish the first leg of our trip, say nothing about attempting the second or climbing up to where the elk was lying, and he certainly would never carry a pack of meat back down all the way to camp! I was really just concerned about how we'd even get him back to camp!

It was Ross who finally said we should just go get the elk down and not worry about him; he'd just have to stay there until we returned. We all gathered around and prayed for Ross, then headed down the trail knowing that this meant we'd all have to work a lot harder. We believed we could do it, but Ross was really our main concern.

We were about halfway up our second leg when there was a sudden commotion coming from behind us. It was Ross, catching up to us and even passing us on the slippery trail! I absolutely couldn't believe what I was seeing. I don't ever recall big Ross passing me on any climb, even when he was in his best condition; now he was passing me after having his back go completely out on him! When we finally got him to slow down and pull over to the side of the trail, we asked him what had happened to bring about such a miraculous change.

Ross said he was just lying there after we left, knowing that his back could not take any more abuse. Physically and emotionally he was feeling totally wiped out, like this trip was just too much to endure in his own strength. He was finished. It was in that state that he finally just breathed out this simple prayer, releasing everything to the Lord's hands: "Jesus, I can't do this anymore. You are going to have to take over and heal me and give me the strength I need." Then he said he kind of passed out for a while. When he came to, all the pain and tightness in his back was completely gone. At first he couldn't believe it, but then he decided he might as well try to get up and just see what would happen. So, he got back up on his feet. There was no pain! He turned from one side to the other and stretched out a little, and to his delight, there was no sign of any back problems at all!

We all stood by the side of the creek feeling amazed by what had just happened and I think we started to recall some other great things the Lord had accomplished in our elk camps in the past. It was really a unique and special moment for all of us, and I don't think any of us who were standing on that holy ground that day walked away unchanged in our own personal faith in Jesus Christ.

Even now as I recall the incident, I remember the overwhelming sense of wonder and awe that came over me because of what the Lord had accomplished. It was as if we had come all the way up to the mountain just for that moment, so the Lord could infuse all of us with new faith and new confidence in Him. We thought we were just there to hunt elk, but He had a bigger plan in mind.

I'll have to admit, I was wondering if the healing would hold under all the stress we would be putting it under, and I wondered whether Ross would really be able to complete the tough journey. But, to everyone's amazement and joy, he not only completed the job, he led the way through most of it.

Moreover, he completed the week without any further back complications at all.

In 2014, four of us headed out together on opening day of the muzzleloader season including my son, David, his buddy Kyle, my friend, Carroll, and myself. We had one muzzleloader tag and two archery tags. I was along to do the calling. From early on I noticed that Carroll was having a tough time keeping up. He's the kind of guy who never complains, so I really thought that he was just a bit out of shape and wore out from packing in the day before up to camp. This was Carroll's second time hunting with us, and even on our first hunt he would put his head down and just slowly bull doze his way up the tough climbs. But this time by afternoon he was laying on the ground and looking physically stressed.

When I asked Carroll what was going on, he told me that his heart was out of rhythm, but he had dealt with this problem for many years and he knew how to get it back into rhythm. He took off his shoes and socks and stood on cold rocks to somehow jolt his heart beat, but this time it didn't work. I really started to get concerned when he took off his shirt and laid on the rocks! He laid there for 30 minutes and still nothing changed. He seemed sluggish and tired. I don't like to ever just sit around without doing some calling, so I bugled and a bull responded, so we all started going after this bull that was on the other side of the canyon. David and Kyle were working hard to get out in front of me, and Carroll did his best, but when we finally got really close to the bull Carroll told me he couldn't go any further. I started to think, "Rescue mission." Carroll is what I would call a "Die-hard" hunter. He will endure the elements and go until he drops in pursuit of big game, so when I saw him laying on the ground when a herd bull was less than 300 yards away and still bugling, I became very concerned and started to wonder if we were going to get him safely back to camp and after that, to a hospital.

Nobody got a shot at the bull and he eventually disappeared out of hearing range, so we started making our way down to the creek bottom and the trail back to camp. Carroll would walk maybe 30 yards, and he would have to stop and try to catch his breath. I wouldn't have thought anything of that except that we were going downhill. When we got to a small meadow, I bugled, and immediately had a response from a fast moving bull that was coming down the mountainside toward us. The guys all set up, hoping the bull would step out into the meadow (which is very rare on the public land we hunt this time of the year), but he skirted the meadow again and continued his race down to the lower meadows.

It was going to be a long slow walk back to camp, in fact I think it was midnight before we made it. I prayed for Carroll while David was getting some water out of the creek, but there didn't seem to be any change. Carroll struggled so much going up even the slightest grades that David and Kyle had to get under his arms, lift him up, and carry him up the hill. Even with that help he would have to stop after a short distance to catch his breath. By now, I had no doubt that I would be trying to get him to a hospital or even trying to call in a rescue helicopter if he made it back to camp.

While he was resting, I called David and Kyle over to where Carroll was standing and said, "We need to all pray for him together." Everybody was quick to agree, so we prayed and then continued our journey. A few minutes later, Carroll was walking on his own effortlessly. He said that it took about 30 yards after praying and his heart suddenly went back into rhythm. There was no doubt in his mind that God had touched his heart miraculously. The next two days he stayed closer to camp just to rest his body, but on Wednesday morning he was climbing back up into the high country with us. That evening David and I called in a 320" class 6x6 that he harvested.

I have had several experiences when bulls reacted as if we were a small herd of cows coming down through the timber in the evening making cow calls. We have gotten really close to some really fired up bulls that way, but I really never knew what more to do to harvest one. On this night I had a plan. As we got off course just a little bit, we came through some really thick timber and we made a lot of noise and a bull let out a scream. He was really close (within 150 yards), so I quickly motioned for Carroll to set up in a very small shooting lane, and I watched as the other two quickly split up to sit above and below him. I quickly turned and walked away from the bull while continuing to break as many branches as I could with my feet. I also cow called to draw the bull past the shooters. The bull went crazy and let out a full bugle with chuckles. He was less than 75 yards away now and screaming as loud as he could, which certainly put pour Carroll's heart under intense pressure!

All of a sudden David was with me calling. He had an arrow in his bow, but he was breaking branches and cow calling with me. I said, "What are you doing?" He excitedly said, "Break as many branches as you can!" and he cow called again. I was a bit confused, but later he said that he had watched three hunters in a video all cow calling together and the variety of calls seemed to help call the bull in, so he wanted to help Carroll get this bull. It was a very selfless act of teamwork for sure because where he would have been sitting is right where the bull ended up when Carroll shot. I think the opening day crisis had David believing this might be Carroll's last chance to get his first bull. But Carroll's heart gave him no trouble on that day or the next when we came back to cut up the big bull and hall it down. In fact, he had no further problems with his heart that week.

There are times when we pray for a healing and nothing seems to happen and sometimes it simply means we need to pray again. Or there are other times when we pray and go to a doctor for help and still little or nothing seems to happen in the physical. But I believe that incidents like these are meant to be shared so that we don't just give up on God's healing power. And so that everyone's faith is increased and all of our eyes are turned toward the one who is able to do much more than we could ever ask or think—even in an elk camp.

See "Think It Through" – page 86

9 Faith

I was up on the side of "Bull Hill," when suddenly I heard the faint sound of footsteps, and out of the corner of my eye I saw a bull elk coming right toward me. It was early morning and I had been doing some cow calling and bugling in a location that was very close to where I had shot my first bull. But on this morning I heard no replies and had no idea that any elk were in the area. Of course, just because you don't see or hear anything is not a reason to relax your hunting instincts. The best strategy for hunting elk is to assume that there may be a bull behind every tree. Be very quiet when you are still hunting, use your ears and eyes to your best advantage, and watch the wind currents diligently.

As I slowly turned my head to get a better look at what I heard coming my way, the bull took a few more steps, then looked in my direction and stopped dead in his tracks only 30 yards away. That was just enough time for me to confirm that it was a legal bull and get my gun up and ready to fire. Sure it sounds like a great shot opportunity for me, but not perfect as the bull had chosen to stop quartering toward me with his front shoulder behind a tree. I had a choice between an angle shot at his front chest or his neck, neither of which I was really crazy about. The best shot with a muzzleloader is always straight through both lungs. We have lost bulls that were hit in the front shoulder before, and I have lost deer that were hit in the neck. The problem in my opinion is that you may hit only one lung if you shoot for the chest and you may miss all of the major blood vessels and the vertebrate if you shoot for the neck. So, on this particular day with only seconds to decide before the bull turned and fled, I opted for getting at least one lung, so I aimed for the chest and fired.

I wish I could say the bull dropped within 100 yards, or 200 yards, or even 300 yards, but he didn't. Paul and Joe heard my shot and came to investigate what had happened. We started following the blood trail as it led us downhill, but after 200 yards the trail seemed to be drying up, so we decided to stop and give the animal an hour or two to lie down. There was no question that he was going to go down; the problem is that an elk can cover a lot of ground in a short amount of time with his very long legs.

What we did next, I have no doubt, made the difference between recovering the animal and losing it. This may be hard for you to believe, but we stopped, recognized our need for help, and prayed for God's guidance to direct our steps to that bull. It's not like we weren't experienced trackers because all of us are bow hunters and have had plenty of opportunities to track wounded deer. We knew all about following gut shot deer that leave little more than a drop of blood every five to ten yards and aren't heavy enough to leave a track. Several times I personally have successfully tracked down deer whose trail fit that description.

After our break was over, we got back on the trail, which took us up a short but very steep familiar ridge that was about 30 feet high and led up to some very thick cover my first bull had lost us in. The signs of blood were becoming so rare that all we could do was to try and locate the bull's track. We would constantly wander off the trail and then one of us would find a drop of blood and get us all back on the trail. At one point, I remember looking at Joe, and he just shrugged his shoulders as if to say, "I'm clueless!" That was also when he informed me that he was color-blind. That didn't help me at all because I was already feeling clueless and anxious myself!

Joe stuck right behind Paul after he made some comment about having the guidance we needed to find the bull. I was a bit reluctant because I couldn't see any trail left behind by our elk at all. There were tracks left by some other elk in the small amount of dirt we found in between the weeds and brush, but it seemed impossible to differentiate our bull's track from the other tracks. But Paul seemed confident that the Lord was giving him the guidance we needed. He told us he didn't understand it, but he just knew internally where to go! He said, "I've got this one," and on he went like a dog on a scent trail with two men in tow!

At one point especially I questioned if he were really on the right trail, so I let him go ahead while I searched the ground on my hands and knees for more signs. When I found nothing, I called them on the radio and his response was simply, "Come on down toward the creek." So off I went, hoping that he knew what he was doing.

As soon as we crossed the creek, we spotted a little blood on the ground. That was the first blood any of us had seen in a long time, and I can't tell you how relieved we were to find it. I know that there are a lot of hunters who would have given up the search long before they got to that point, but we were committed to searching until everybody agreed it was absolutely hopeless. In this case, Paul never even considered giving up because he felt he had a divine Guide showing him just enough to keep us on track, inch by inch and no more or less.

But now the blood trail became a little easier to find so we were able to pick up the pace. We followed it uphill for about 200 yards into a thicker area that looked like a good potential place for a bed, and there we found the bull. He was still alive but too weak to get up.

What a relief to recover that bull! We all knew that we had successfully tracked it for almost half a mile (according to the GPS), on little more than a few drops of blood, a few tracks, a prayer, and a faith in what I call "GGS"- God's Guidance System.

I hope this story helps you see that faith is not a small, intangible, uncertain, mysterious thing that you only use when you're in church. Faith in God's ability to guide our lives in our everyday decisions or in a crisis is available if we really need it and seek for it. Don't wait for eternity to discover that He can safely get you to where you need to be. Now you know why I said that stopping to pray was what made the difference between success and failure. But you don't have to just take my word for it; seek after it for your own life and discover for yourself what can happen, even on an elk hunt.

See "Think It Through" – page 87

10 THE LITTLE FOXES

Joe was suddenly within ten yards of a very large bull that had seemingly come out of nowhere, stepped into the small opening in the brush where we were calling from and was now standing broadside. I was sitting about ten yards behind Joe, and I had just completed my first bugle not more than sixty seconds before this big old bull elk appeared and positioned himself perfectly for Joe's arrow. At first, I didn't think that my partner had even seen the animal come in because he was watching a different opening, so I softly called Joe's name, but even as I did that, Joe spotted the bull and slowly turned himself for an easy shot.

It had been a great hunt already with several close encounters with the bow, but as the old adage says, "Close only counts in hand grenades and horseshoes," and definitely not archery hunting. We had hunted our way far back into a heavily forested mountain canyon, bugling about every 100 yards whenever we saw a lot of elk sign. I have a little adage that I made up and use a lot when I'm hunting elk, I like to say, "It's better to bugle than to bust a bull." By bugling you at least open the door that will give the bull the opportunity to respond with a return bugle, letting you know he's in the area. But if you bust him, he's gone and you'll probably have no chance! We climbed a large rock outcropping, set up and bugled several times, waited five to ten minutes or so for a response, then took out our cameras and captured some great pictures of the beautiful mountain scenery.

It was time to get back to our hunt, so Joe and I quietly made our way into the thick forest on a five-foot wide trail left by loggers maybe 100 years before. There was elk sign everywhere, so we walked only about 40 yards and entered into a 15-foot wide opening. We decided to set up to bugle again, but this time the prize we had been looking for showed up.

I watched as Joe slowly moved just two or three steps to get around some brush that was between him and the elk, draw back his bow, carefully aim at the bull's side, and release the arrow. It's important to understand that Joe is the kind of guy who buys the very top-of-the-line equipment, practices shooting until everything is right, and has the experience of killing numerous whitetail deer in Wisconsin with his bow. He's a successful hunter with a bow and arrow partly because he is a detail person and a bit of a perfectionist. Every hunter finds out sooner or later that there's another old adage that is really true, "The devil is in the details," and Joe is one of those guys who really lives by it. He and his dad and brothers have harvested many trophy Whitetails because they know that "Murphy's law" is also true, "If anything can go wrong, it will!" And, Murphy was an optimist!

When Joe released his arrow, the big bull spun around and charged out of the set up area faster than you would ever think an animal that size could move. I was a bit unsure of exactly what had happened with the shot. It sure seemed like the arrow had hit the ground beneath the elk, but I wasn't totally sure if it had gone through the bull before it hit the dirt. It also seemed impossible that Joe could have missed at such a close range, so I threw my hands into the air as if to ask, "What happened?" He answered all my questions when he pointed at a tiny little twig that was hanging down, unseen and unnoticed in front of where his arrow had flown, deflecting it just enough to miss its intended mark. When I say tiny twig, I mean it was no more than an eighth of an inch in diameter, so small I couldn't believe it could have had the effect it did when the bull was so close. But there was absolutely no doubt that it had destroyed Joe's opportunity to harvest his first bull with a bow.

I'll never forget the look on Joe's face, it was a look of total disappointment and the expression of someone who was feeling totally discouraged and defeated. How could something so small ruin such an easy shot? He was so close! We both knew from experience that it doesn't take much to deflect an arrow, but at that particular moment, we had to deal with the fact that we had come so far, spent so much time and money preparing for this perfect opportunity, and a single tiny twig had stolen success right out of our hands. How could that have happened?

My response was to quickly bugle again in the hope that the bull might turn around. After all, he hadn't gotten wind of us or had a good look at us; he just knew that something was wrong. That quickly forced both of us to forget the twig, at least for the moment, and within five minutes we had another bull come in to very close range, twice! He got too close the first time, got nervous and jumped back into the brush. So I called again and he came back in, but the brush where he was standing was too thick again for a shot with an arrow, and the bull refused to take that all too common "one more step" which would have put him in the shooting lane for Joe.

So, we were back to having to deal with the twig deflection again, which now seemed even more disappointing since our second opportunity did not work out either. Sure, we talked it out. We are men, right! With archery it is one of those things you learn to deal with. But to tell you the whole truth, to this very day, I'm still perturbed with how something so small could have destroyed such a perfect set up to harvest such a big bull elk! It reminded me of something a wise man named Solomon wrote in the Bible, he said "It's the little foxes that destroy the vine" (Song of Solomon 2:15).

See "Think It Through" – page 88

11 COMPROMISE

It was an hour before first light and Bob, Paul, and I were climbing up the first and steepest part of our day's hunt in the Colorado Mountains. We slowly made our way up through the timber to about 9,900 feet in elevation.

Paul and I had already tagged our bulls, so we were doing some calling for Bob, the oldest member of our group at roughly sixty years of age. Bob was breathing hard and sweating profusely, but he is a tough man and he refused to quit climbing up through the timber in pursuit of his first bull.

Just after we entered a notably thicker area we thought might be productive, we spotted a bull in front of us. It was slowly making its way up to a bedding area, but it was just a spike. In our area of Colorado, a bull must be four points on one side or have at least one five-inch eye guard. As we entered the thicker cover, we began to see a lot of bull antler rubs on the sides of trees. A big bull can make a rub nearly ten feet high, and some of the rubs we were seeing were very high, very wide and very deep.

When we bugle, we always set up first by sending the shooter out in front of the caller by at least 50 yards, and 100 yards is even better depending on the thickness of the cover. The reason for this is a bull will often "hang-up" at a certain distance from the bugler, so if the shooter is up in front of him, he's more likely to have an opportunity to shoot. The wind is always a challenge in the mountains, so we use small plastic squeeze bottles filled with chalk. A puff of powdered chalk is light enough to show us even the slightest air movement, and we use these often because of the constantly changing wind currents. Today you can buy these little bottles in sports shops for a couple of dollars. It will be one of your best elk hunting investments.

We set up and I gave my usual short, high pitched, one- or two- note bugle to imitate a small bull, and immediately had a response from a bull not more than 150 yards away. Normally, if you can hear a bugle in thick cover, he is closer than you think. This wasn't one of those high pitched, squeaky bugles that are sometimes associated with smaller bulls; this was a strong, multi-noted growl from the boss.

We waited for a few minutes, checked the wind, and made a bold move directly toward the bull, making sure we wouldn't bump him as we quickly stalked in. We set up again and this time I gave a stronger and longer bugle in an effort to challenge the bull and get him worked up. He responded immediately, and we knew the distance had been cut in half or more because the bull sounded very close and very agitated. The aggressive way he was responding told me he was probably going to come in very close.

We closed the distance to maybe 50 yards and set up again, this time bugling with even more intensity to let this big boy know, "We are moving in on your turf." The bull responded immediately, but this time his bugle revealed he was moving downwind of us, so I quickly sprayed elk scent into the air and on every branch or tree near me in an effort to try and camouflage our scent. I waited for a few minutes, but the bull remained quiet, so I picked up a branch and started aggressively rubbing it against a tree, even breaking off branches in an effort to try and imitate an angry bull raking a tree with its antlers.

That was all it took, the big bull couldn't resist the challenge any longer and moved within 15 yards of Bob and Paul, who in turn were only 15 yards in front of me. I don't like being that close to the shooter, but everything was happening so fast and the cover was so thick that it just kind of worked out that way. Bob had his muzzleloader up and ready for the shot, and I watched and waited for the explosion of smoke and noise; but instead, all I heard was the muzzleloaders dreaded "click."

We had been having a lot of wet weather, experiencing everything from rain, snow, sleet, freezing rain, to even what I call ice pellets. Every possible form of precipitation can be expected in the high mountain country, even in September. The best strategy with muzzleloading in wet weather is to discharge your gun every night, keep it dry overnight, and carefully reload in the morning. When there are periods of on and off precipitation, it's easy to forget to discharge your gun and assume that all is well when it is not.

Apparently Bob's musket cap or powder had gotten damp enough to misfire, then when Bob tried to quickly replace the ignition cap after the misfire, the bull heard the clicking noise and knew something was wrong. He turned and fled in a big hurry, and there was no way I could call him back in. He was now a much more educated bull than when our drama began. We had failed to take this trophy because of a small compromise in powder and ignition integrity. To this day Bob talks about the disappointment he felt when his gun failed to fire.

Several years before this on our very first hunting trip to Colorado, Dan and I were hunting together in a heavy snowfall. Each snowflake seemed as big as a Frisbee floating down from the heavens. We came across some very fresh tracks, and because I was carrying a cow tag, we decided to attempt following the elk until we had the opportunity for a shot.

The small group of elk took us up and down through the thick undercover until our light began to fade. We knew we were running out of time, so we quickly dropped down to a creek and small meadow, thinking the elk were headed in that general direction. Sure enough, the elk were just in front of us, moving into the meadow when we arrived there.

When I purchased my first muzzleloader, the in-line models were just coming out. Even though they had proven to be more reliable in challenging weather, I decided to buy a side-hammer style gun in stainless steel. The only reason I did this was I thought the side-hammer design fit in better with the whole idea of this primitive style hunt like the mountain men of old. What I didn't realize was that little decision would cost me my first black powder elk.

Through the heavy snowfall I suddenly saw the head of a large cow reaching high up into a spruce tree. I don't think it was more than 50 yards away, so I pointed it out to Dan, took my safety off, and got ready for a shot. Moments later one of the cows walked across the narrow opening to the meadow, so I aimed just behind the front shoulder and squeezed the trigger.

What happened next is something black powder hunters call a "hang-fire." Fire from the tiny #11 percussion cap is supposed to travel down through a narrow passageway leading into the breach of the gun and igniting the powder. Under damp conditions however, the ignition may be slowed causing a "hang-fire." For me on that damp snowy evening, the result was a wounded elk, hit in the back leg, about one step back from where I had aimed.

Dan and I trailed the elk a short distance, but it was getting dark and the elk was still moving. There wasn't a good blood trail even though the snow had just let up, so we decided not to push the wounded elk but come back the next morning. Our hope was that the animal would lie down before it went very far.

We returned early the next day and by examining the tracks soon discovered that the elk was dragging its rear leg. The elk's trail took us steadily higher, and like an Energizer battery, that elk just kept "going and going and going!" It didn't help that we came upon coyote tracks on top of our elk's tracks and he was pushing it in his attempt to hunt down our cow as well. The tracks showed what looked like an encounter between the two of them, but the coyote apparently decided this elk wasn't anywhere close to dying.

So after several hours of tracking, it became clear that this elk was going to out climb and outrun all of us, and we were forced to give up the chase. It was certainly a big disappointment after we had invested so much time and energy in the hope that we'd be able to harvest this animal, but it just wasn't going to happen.

To this day, I believe that a big reason why I failed to harvest that animal was because of my decision to buy a side-hammer rifle. Sure, after I got home and told "Cabela's" what had happened they understood and graciously exchanged that gun for a brand new in-line rifle; but, it was too late for that hunting trip, and I never did fill that elk tag.

The good news is the new in-line rifle has never failed me to this day. I think you would agree that my experience emphasizes the point that settling for second best, which we may define as compromising, will eventually bring unfavorable consequences.

See "Think It Through" – page 89

12 SELFISHNESS

Randy and I were on top of "Bull Hill" when we finally heard an elk's bugle echo through the morning air in reply to my call. It was 2007, the muzzleloader season had started during the first week of September, and what happened to me on that day is probably going to sound totally unbelievable. The Colorado temperatures in the high country were in the low 70's. Although it was too early in the season and too warm for most of the bulls to begin their bugling ritual, we had located one bull that was responding.

It soon became apparent that the bull was not coming in to our bugle or cow call attempts, so we quickly moved in the general direction of the elk, making sure that we stayed above the animal in elevation. We did this for two reasons: first, because the warming air thermals would soon begin to rise and carry our scent right to the nose of any animal that was on the alert above us; and second, because generally a bull is more responsive to a challenge that comes from the same elevation or from above it.

We chose the more conservative approach of staying above the bull rather than moving directly down toward it in an effort to challenge it into a standoff and confrontation. I am not sure exactly why we chose this stationary tactic, because I usually prefer to take a more aggressive approach with a bull that has returned two or three bugles without hesitation. But after we had walked two to three hundred yards, we began to bump into other elk that were hanging close to the bull, which seemed to indicate that we were pursuing a herd bull.

Earlier in the season, I believe the older bulls are generally more responsive than satellite bulls. They seem to know first that the season for mating is coming, and the rag-horned younger bulls start to figure it out later. After what seemed like an hour of calling and trying to stay with the traveling bull, we could finally tell from his bugle that we were no more than 150 yards directly above it, and he had stopped moving higher. As we tried to move toward it we bumped several more cows that quickly fled and ran straight down in the bull's direction. But fortunately the wind currents were moving uphill by now, which meant that the animals couldn't get our scent.

At this point, Randy and I were undecided about exactly what to do next. This was our first big encounter of the season with a bugling bull, and we didn't want to blow our chances by spooking the bull as we attempted to approach it on the noisy, dry, forest floor on which we had already busted several other elk. So, we elected to sit tight for a while and just be patient and see what opportunities would appear. Occasionally we would bugle and he would respond back with a bugle, but he wouldn't move toward us. We tried to cow call also but had no response. At about noon, something happened that we have found to be common among herd bulls, he got up, bugled, and took off on a survey of the entire side of the mountain presumably looking for more cows!

After he had bugled twice and moved to our left, I thought he had moved only about a hundred yards so we might have an opportunity to aggressively pursue the animal and attempt to challenge it into an encounter. I told Randy that we needed to move fast! But just as soon as we had put on our fanny packs, we heard the bull bugle again, this time high above us! He had ascended so quickly and covered so much ground that it just seemed impossible.

All we could do was drop our packs and wait and see what the bull would do next. I call this kind of behavior, "cruising," when for some unknown reason to me bulls just get totally crazy! I think they're working on rounding up their herd, but they sure don't give any cows they locate any time to keep up with them. I really felt that if he was a herd bull, he would want to return to the remaining cows that were below us, and we were now positioned directly between him and his herd. We each had an open area through which we could shoot that ran parallel with the side of the mountain. That would certainly extend our range of sight in the thick forest cover, so we sat down and waited to see if the bull would return. To our delight, he did.

Earlier, when we first arrived at our camp, I was feeling a little apprehensive about having the others rely on me to do most of the calling for them. No one had said anything to that effect, it was just a battle I was having within myself. I had not had a tag the last two times we had traveled west to hunt, but I went along exclusively to call and help others get a bull. But this time, I did have a license and wanted to get a bull as much as anyone else.

My partner that day, Randy, is the kind of man that seems to have an unlimited supply of patience, grace and mercy for other people. He certainly wanted to get an elk and fill his own tag, but he would have been happy to see me get one too. He's a short, stocky, and very strong guy with a big sense of humor and a good amount of humility. I'm not saying he doesn't have a competitive spirit, because he certainly proved that he does one day during our Whitetail deer hunting season.

Neither of us had harvested a buck and the nine day season was well over half gone. Randy was sitting in my usual stand and I was in Paul's stand because he had taken a buck. It was nine o'clock in the morning when I heard a buck grunting in the thick willow brush in front of me. I got a couple of glimpses of it and confirmed that it was a big buck, but no shot opportunities opened up. Meanwhile, Randy had given up, gotten out of his stand and was crossing the marsh out in front of me on his way to his truck just as the buck came into view. The buck stopped, looked right up at me in the stand, and revealed the bright white patch under it's chin. My crosshairs fell on that white patch as I squeezed the trigger and the deer immediately went down. Randy just changed his course when he heard me shoot and came to see my trophy. All he said to me was, "You Potlicker!" We still laugh about that comment.

At my suggestion, Randy and I flipped a coin over who would get to set up for the first encounter when we started our elk hunt. I won and he was very okay with that. But so far we had only called in one bull, a silent bull that I had called in for Randy. But he had only seen it briefly and did not get a good opportunity for a shot. So I was feeling more anxious all the time about getting an opportunity to fill my tag. I wanted Randy and the others to get an elk too, and I would do my best to help them. But what I didn't recognize at the time that I was really more concerned about myself than about the others.

Now things were really starting to get a little crazy. As we sat there waiting to see what would happen, I suddenly had this strange thought come across my mind: "Don't be selfish and I'll give you a big blessing." At first I didn't know what to think about it; was this me and my own weird thoughts or was this God trying to tell me something? Some people don't believe that an Almighty God has the time to talk to us little people about such trivial things. But I decided that if this was God's Spirit speaking to me, He would not just drop that thought into my mind one time and let it go. He knows I'm a little slow in picking up on His intuitive words within my heart. He would continue to impress me with making a choice, and that is what happened. Over and over again, I heard that same message inside my heart: "Don't be selfish and I'll give you a big blessing."

I can't say I understood what it all meant, but it doesn't take a rocket scientist to figure out that someone was trying to tell me that my thinking was self-centered and I needed to change it. What I didn't know was that I was about to face a test that, if I passed, would include a reward that would be much bigger and come much sooner than I could have ever anticipated.

At 1:15 p.m., we suddenly heard the bull coming down the mountain moving directly toward us just as we had hoped. His angle of descent was taking him just behind me in Randy's viewing area, so I quickly but silently reversed my position so that I could possibly get a shot also. Within about a minute, branches began breaking not more than fifty yards away as the bull busted his way through the heavy timber, weaving his antlers through the branches with the finesse of a true trophy.

When Randy heard how close the bull was and how quickly it was coming, he got up and moved to get a better shot, accidentally knocking his plastic water bottle against a big tree stump. That sound of crunching plastic effectively warned the elk that something was wrong. You can get away with a lot of natural noises when you're hunting elk, but any human noises (like plastic or metal sounds) are going to send him running. The bull immediately stopped in his tracks, listened, changed his course, and headed directly away from us.

At first I couldn't believe Randy had just busted this perfect setup! How could he, a very experienced and successful hunter, have blown this? That's when the words came back to my heart, "Don't be selfish and I'll give you a big blessing." Suddenly it hit me, I was being critical of Randy and my criticism was based on nothing but my own selfishness. How did God know that I was going to do that? I could hide it or dress it up and camouflage it and make it appear to be something more attractive, but it was still criticism based in selfishness. I believe that this was my test, to see if I would keep my criticism to myself and my big mouth shut. I could see that Randy was obviously as disappointed as I was, and he didn't need to hear me rub it in; so, I decided I would keep my mouth shut and wait and see what the Lord would do in response to his promise to send a "big blessing."

The bull avoided us and I moved about ten yards to a position with some shooting lanes looking down through the timber in the direction of where the bull had been lying. Judging from the bugling that followed, we heard the bull descend below us then circle back up toward his previous position near his cows. That's when the thought hit me that I should try a loud and sharp hyper cow call and just see what happens. I didn't normally use that call at that time, but I decided I might as well try something different! Many years later I heard a cow hyper calling to me after I bugled. She called over and over again as if she was saying, "Come over here and get me you big hunk of a bull!" It's become a call I use often for herd bulls.

So I gave one hyper cow call and sat back to see if anything would happen. Almost immediately I could hear the bull moving, breaking branches, and getting closer. I could hear his antlers hitting undergrowth as he made his way up toward me. I couldn't believe this was happening, especially since that bull knew a strange sound had come from that location. I kept thinking about what I believed the Lord had promised me if I controlled my selfish criticalness, and it was really happening! I wouldn't blame anybody for not believing this story, but this is exactly what happened! The God of all creation was really sending this "big blessing" to me! He really does have control over all His creation! I am sure that many hunters have prayed and asked God to send an animal to them, but for me on that day, it was really happening!

I had to quietly turn to my right as the bull came steadily closer, and I put my gun up on my knee and got ready for a shot. I could hear elk chirping below me and I thought it was cows chirping at the bull; instead, it was the bull that was doing this loud, sharp chirping. He was definitely chirping at me, the hyper cow that called to him from above! I was absolutely in disbelief when suddenly his huge head appeared between two large trees that were no more than 30 yards away.

The opening in the trees was no more than 14 inches wide and the bull was quartering toward me. When his huge chest and front shoulder came into view, I saw an opportunity for a good shot just in front of the right shoulder, angling into his heart and lungs. I took careful aim and pulled the trigger, sending a cloud of smoke and a deadly bullet in his direction.

There is always a risk of an elk catching a circling wind current on these mountain slopes, so sometimes it is best to take the first good opportunity you have for a shot. I was very confident in my shot, and to this day I clearly recall seeing my glowing sight focused on the left side of his chest as I pulled the trigger. The Lord had fulfilled his promise of sending a "big blessing" to me, and I was given a huge opportunity that day, but in the end we discovered that my shot was not perfect.

We had a problem, we couldn't find a drop of blood on the ground and the only sign of a hit was some short brown hair lying on the ground, which seemed to indicate that the bullet had only grazed his leg. We searched for several hours and never saw any sign that the animal was wounded in any way. In the end we never recovered the bull. This was very confusing to me at the time because I believed this elk was a special gift from God. There was absolutely no doubt in my mind that God Himself had sent it to me, so how could I go wrong? How could I not get it?

Only afterward did I begin to understand that God often sends blessings to us, He's given us many "great and precious promises," according to 2 Peter 1:4 in the Bible, but what we do with them and how we handle them is our responsibility. The Lord showed me that he had indeed fulfilled His promise, and the rest was up to me. In hindsight, I should have waited for a better shot, one where no branches could deflect my bullet, where I had a wider window to shoot through, and a standing elk to shoot at. I guess "bull fever" got the best of me.

The good news is that just two days later I had a second opportunity to call in what I believe was this same herd bull. In a bugling sequence that lasted nearly three hours and brought Paul's son Nathan, to within fifteen yards of this trophy, God gave me another opportunity to lay down my selfishness and give someone else a chance at this "big blessing." This was Nathan's very first elk hunt, and he excitedly told me that the bull was so huge that the cattle in their barn seemed small in comparison.

Although what happened in this heart pumping hunt is material for another chapter some day, I can tell you that in the end I felt like I had gained a real spiritual trophy in experiencing God's mighty hand over the animal kingdom just like Jesus' disciples experienced in John 21. I had also come to recognize my own criticalness, that in His eyes selfishness and criticism are related, and that He will reward those who defeat them.

See "Think It Through" – page 90

13 GOALS

"Should I bugle again?" I asked my son, David, as we and his buddy Kyle were hunting our way back down off the mountain toward our elk camp. It was late in the afternoon of our first day of muzzleloader season in Colorado. "What for?" he answered in a rather negative and pessimistic tone as if he thought our chances of seeing an elk were finished and the day's hunt was over. I bugled again anyway with my typical high pitched and short bugle and immediately a bull responded below us not more than 200 yards away. The chase was on!

This hunt, on September 11 of 2011, was to become the culmination of nearly thirty years of learning how to call and hunt bull elk for me, and it would become the climax of four hunting trips for my son David.

I had already successfully called in many bulls for my son on two archery hunts and one muzzleloader hunt, but he had yet to harvest a bull; although he did successfully harvest a cow on the last day of our last archery hunt. All the previous hunts had become less about harvesting an animal and more about teaching him how to hunt and what to do in various situations.

Some of the things I learned in my thirty years of hunting and wanted to teach him were:

1. How far away from the bugler should the shooter setup in thick cover? What about open cover? We had always hunted on public land in the National Forest where there is greater hunting pressure, so we learned to have the shooter setup at least 50 yards away, and 100 yards in more open forest. We never setup in an open area because the bulls we hunt just never seem to walk in to the open, they always were in the thickest cover around us.

2. What should we look for in trying to find the right place to set up? With archery especially, but muzzleloader also, it's always about finding shooting lanes in several different directions.

3. What about the wind? In the mountains a temperature current is always driving a wind, the thermo drops in the early morning and late evening and rises when the temperature begins to increase. Plus, we need to accommodate ourselves to the prevailing wind and the never ending circular motion of wind currents. The only hope of beating the wind is to carry a wind detector and use it constantly.

4. How close should we try to get to a bull that has responded to a couple of bugles? Just sitting there and waiting for the bull to come closer to you after a bugle or two can be a self-defeating strategy, depending on the mood of the bull. Once a bull has responded to a couple of my calls, I like to move in fast and try to get within a hundred yards of him, depending on the thickness of the cover, before I bugle again. When I say quickly, I mean we are literally running sometimes, and noise is not always an issue because bulls often make a lot of noise when they are on the move. However, if the bull's response to my next bugle indicates that he is still on the move, then I will quickly move toward him again and try to get within a hundred yards of where I think he is positioned before I bugle again, and the closer, the better.

Once a bull has stopped and is ready to confront, he will often start rubbing a tree, and that is your chance to try to stalk into range. You have to try to figure out the exact mood he's in, then make or don't make a move. I doubt that there is anybody who guesses right every time, so sometimes you have to be willing to take a risk, and try getting closer. But that can be an unnerving and tense move to stalk closer to a wild, screaming, angry bull! You have to force yourself to move as close as you think you can without being detected. David was about to prove whether or not he had learned the lessons well.

I remember one time when David was calling for me on an archery hunt, and it was one of those stubborn bulls that just refused to come toward us. As it turned out, he was with some cows which is frequently a reason why bulls don't want to come to a call. The wind had switched and the bull stopped bugling so we thought he had left town, but we just patiently waited for a while, then bugled again after ten or fifteen minutes, and he responded. The bull was not far away, I would guess he was less than 100 yards, but we were in some pretty thick stuff so it's often hard to guess it right.

The bull was above me so I started inching my way up and David had learned to follow me silently with the bugle and stay at least 50 yards back. I knew I was getting very close because I could hear his little whimpers and squeals and I could tell he was on the move. I wasn't shaking but I really had to force myself to edge closer because my nerves were really on edge. Moving felt like the hardest thing I had ever done. I spotted a cow and had a clear shot at her, I had a license for a cow or a bull, but she wasn't what I was after. Suddenly the bull appeared as he made his way through the brush no more than 20 yards away. I couldn't get a clear shot even at that close range and his patience ran out very quickly, in a few seconds he busted and was gone.

So, when this bull in 2011 responded to the call, the three of us, David, his buddy Kyle, and I all looked at each other with raised eye brows and excited gestures and quickly moved closer to where the bull had bugled. I bugled again when I thought we were well within 100 yards and he instantly responded with a bugle. Now we knew which direction he was going and how close he was. The boys wanted me to immediately bugle again and try to get him to come back to us, but that strategy just didn't feel right to me for this moment. I never like to bugle twice from the same location.

If you think about it, bulls are usually on the move, and it seems like they rarely bugle twice from the same location. Sure they can hang up, and start rubbing a tree after you've got them really worked up, and they'll give a variety of bugles, grunts, and sharp little squeals, but we were only minutes into this encounter. So, we moved again very quickly, and in his direction, knowing that he had dropped over a steep edge that I have labeled, "elk edge" on my GPS.

This wasn't the first time we had encountered elk on this edge. We had run into elk moving up and over it on many occasions in the past; mostly in the mornings, but several times in the evenings as well. When I find these kinds of locations I always lock them into my GPS and label them so that I know what they are. When you are constantly hunting in the timber, it can be impossible to know just exactly where you are, but a GPS removes all the guessing. Instead of just wandering around the mountains, I can focus on locations that were productive in the past and sooner or later it seems to pay off.

I decided to stay back about 50 yards from the edge while I sent the boys up to it. From this location I elected to give some cow calls first just to give the bull a little more incentive to hang around once I knew David and Kyle were set up. David had made a decision to push closer to the bull than he really wanted to go. I think there were too many times in his memory when he failed to push himself closer or he failed to get further away from the caller and an opportunity was missed when a bull "hung up." He had enough encounters under his belt that he now knew instinctively what to do.

He quietly and quickly moved into a small clump of trees and brush, brought his gun up to his shoulder, and froze. From behind David and Kyle I gave a couple of cow calls and the bull immediately screamed back. I could tell he was just on the other side of the edge and was probably waiting for the bull and cows I had fooled him into believing were calling to him.

It was about then that David saw the white tips of this bull's big antlers moving just to his right below him, and he was really close! The bull turned around and stopped behind a big pine tree where David could have taken a shot, but he chose to be patient and wait for a more open shot. I bugled again and the bull started moving into a shooting lane not more than 18 yards from him. He zeroed the open sights just behind the front shoulder, squeezed the trigger, and black powder smoke darkened the sky.

From my location behind a big uprooted tree root I could instantly see where the shot had come from and I watched the smoke rise and then drift down the mountain. I immediately started running toward my son with my fist in the air. It didn't take long to cover the distance and David excitedly began to tell his story after a high five and big hug. There was no doubt in his mind that he had hit the bull hard, it had run down the steep, rocky edge and into the dark timber below. You never know for sure what kind of a search or blood trail you are about to encounter, but it quickly became apparent that this bull wasn't going far.

We quietly made our way down to where the bull had been standing when David shot. It was easy to see where the bull's hooves had dug into the dirt as he spun and ran. Some good blood was also splattered on the rocks. We moved a little lower and peered into the timber with binoculars and just 40 yards or so below us we spotted the bull stumbling in the timber. He fell down, and then stood back up, but looked very shaky.

At first Kyle raised his gun and said he had a shot to finish the bull off, but David wouldn't let him shoot. Instead, David moved in for a shot and pulled the trigger, but the bull didn't move. What we didn't know at the time because of the low light in the dark timber was that we were looking at his rump, and David had just plugged him in the rear. We waited for a short time but the sun was setting by now, so David moved down closer and found a perfect hole for another shot into the bull's side.

I took advantage of this time to climb back up to the top of the ridge, mark the area with flagging tape, and lock in the location on my GPS. It took about a half hour in all for the bull to go down and he never moved more than about 50 yards from where he was first shot. When David came back to get us, his first words to me were, "He's big, dad. He's bigger than your first bull!"

We had a great celebration that included our traditional canned herring meal. Our Wisconsin hunting party had originally started this peculiar form of celebration after we harvested our very first bull taken during a muzzleloader season more than 20 years before. I guess it was all we had left in our fanny pack so we used what we had. And now my son, his buddy and I were joyfully continuing the tradition together.

The big bull's antlers were locked into the tree limbs of a deadfall, so we wrestled them out and spent what was left of the light taking pictures. Then we field dressed it, and forced the body cavity open with a good solid tree branch so it would cool quickly. As an added measure, we wedged some rocks under the bull's body to get it off the ground and help it cool even better.

Then we left as much human scent around the carcass as we could to ward off any hungry predators, and headed back down to camp. The bull was indeed bigger than my biggest, and was the largest we had ever taken. It grossed 318 "Boone and Crocket" points, a great culmination to nearly 30 years of learning how to successfully call in and harvest big bulls at close range, and a great climax for my son's four year pursuit of taking his very first bull.

But that culmination of nearly 30 years of learning took another leap of success when David called in a nice 6 x 6 herd bull for his buddy Kyle just two days later on this same mountainside.

A lot of guys travel west, hire an outfitter and guide who does all the work of finding and calling in the bulls, then brag about what great hunters they are. But my goal was to make it all an adventure, to learn about the elk and how to find and call the animal for myself, to teach my son and others the things I learned so that we could successfully hunt together. And the reason I wrote this book was to help you gain a better understanding of how to harvest one of these magnificent creations of God with your own family or hunting partners in a do-it-yourself hunt. In doing that you will certainly share in the legacy that God has helped me build.

See "Think It Through" – page 91

14 AS GOOD AS IT GETS

It was 12:34 p.m. on the very first day of the 2013 elk muzzleloader season, and I was looking down the barrel of my .50 caliber rifle waiting for the biggest bull I'd ever seen on a hunting trip step into a small opening less than forty yards away. It had been two years since we had been in Colorado hunting elk in 2011, and on that trip my son David had successfully harvested the largest bull any of us had ever taken on the very first day of the season. This was almost starting to become a trend as Nathan, Paul's oldest son, also harvested his first bull on the first morning of our hunt in 2010 on "Bull Hill." Nathan was one very excited hunter on that morning and his dad was one very proud "Papa!" I don't think I bugled more than six times when the bull walked right past Nathan while he was sitting no more than 300 yards above Paul and I.

But now it was September 14, the very latest date possible for the season to open, and yet the aspens had surprised us by still being green. Colorado was experiencing some record rainfall amounts and we had encountered a closed freeway as we attempted to make our way west of Denver. Heavy rains had caused rockslides that shut all westward travel down on Interstate 70. As we got out of our truck to talk with some of the other drivers who were stopped in the lanes next to us, they were also on their way to hunt elk and had been sitting on the freeway since 1 a.m. That was about eight hours ago! There was no telling how long we'd be stuck there.

But just north of Boulder heavy rains had closed mountain roads and west of Loveland flash flood waters coming down from Estes Park were, unknowingly to us, taking personal property and several lives. This was not how we had wanted to start our hunt. Two years ago they were battling fires on the front-range, now it was floods! Elk hunting always seems to be an adventure—that's one of the things that has always drawn me to it.

You have to be ready to face unexpected events and we have even considered ending our hunt early because of an unforeseen crisis. In 2001, when we discovered that New York City had been devastated by an attack, we were all ready to leave if our families needed us. In fact we spent some time together in our tent just praying for our families and for our nation. That certainly wasn't what we had expected to be doing, but it was what we needed to do.

By 10:30 a.m. the highway was reopened and we were on our way to elk camp. When we arrived at our parking spot we were met with another surprise, and this time it was a good one. The flood waters had proved too much for some of the beaver dams and the ones that kept us from crossing at a closer and easier location were gone! That felt like God was blessing us with a special big "Welcome!" sign. I even turned to someone and said, "I really believe God is blessing this trip!" and they immediately agreed. What better way to start a hunting trip than to declare God's blessing over it!

The down-side was that we were going to have to deal with rain every day for the first five days of our eight day hunt. When you are in the mountains, you had better prepare for changing weather conditions or stay home. We backpack everything up five hundred feet to where we set up our camp, so we are trying to stay as light as possible while still being prepared for weather. A good weatherproof and waterproof tent is essential. Warm and light sleeping bags that can handle temperatures in the teens, even in September, are a must. Lightweight boots that are breathable and waterproof are irreplaceable. It may be a clear night and sunny morning, but by the afternoon it can be raining, sleeting, snowing or all of the above. I always carry a tiny little poncho in my fanny pack, and this year I used three of them. Thunderstorms at night and rain and sleet during the day means you have to be ready to keep your powder dry too.

David and I were eagerly up and on our way in the dark on the first morning of our hunt. We knew that the grassy slopes of "Bull Hill" would be super wet, so we elected to head straight up above camp and stay in the dark timber where the grass usually doesn't grow. I had purchased a new GPS with a topography package and was excited to see how it would work. By loading in many of the latitude and longitude numbers I had accumulated in my old but failing GPS, I was able to head for some good locations that had proved valuable in previous years. I was amazed at how accurate the topography map was, and by the end of the week my new GPS had proved to be a great new asset.

We slowly made our way up the mountain while cow calling intermittently every five to ten minutes. Cow calling doesn't often call in an elk, but it does communicate a message that relaxes them. Elk are very vocal animals. When they hear you stepping on sticks that break or knocking your boots on logs you have to climb over, but then hear a cow mew, they think you're just another elk. Of course if they get your scent, things will change dramatically and quickly, so watch the wind and thermal currents constantly.

By late morning you may even feel the thermals change from hitting you on the back of your neck to brushing you in the face as you're moving up. That means you have to change your hunting strategy immediately. Elk love to hang out on the top quarter of a ridge or where the cover is the thickest, so if you are just getting to that point by mid or late morning, your scent may be headed up on a rising thermal straight to the elk. You either have to get above them, or get on the approximate same elevation they are on when you setup and call, but watch for incoming animals to try to get downwind (above you).

By mid morning we started to see some fresh rubs that were just plain big. Whenever we came into an area where there were five to eight rubs close together within about 100 yards, we would set up and Dave would give one short, high pitched bugle. I always tried to get at least fifty yards in front of him and find a location where there were some good shooting lanes. All morning long we slowly made our way up the two miles to the top of the ridge. By late morning we were sitting under trees to get out of the rain and ice pellets. But some of the rubs on trees were so large that we knew there had to be a really big bull somewhere on that mountain. So we didn't really care what the weather was doing, we were feeling motivated to find him.

As we neared the top our stomachs were telling us it was lunch time and a quick look at our watches told us it was almost noon. There was a saddle not far ahead where we had stopped for lunch before, so that was our destination; but, before we headed there, we decided to bugle once into the new flowage on the back side of the ridge we had just topped.

David bugled at 11:55 a.m. and no less than three bulls bugled back. One of them was obviously closer than the others, so we immediately headed down the top of the ridge in his direction. We moved at a pretty fast pace until we had closed the distance in half. Then, just to make sure he was really interested—and to locate his exact position—we bugled again, and he immediately replied with a full set of chuckles.

That was all we needed to know and we all but ran right toward him. My goal is always to get as close to the bull as I possibly can without being seen or winded. Getting within 100 yards in more open conditions or 60 yards in really thick cover can be really nerve racking. The last thing you want to do is bust him, but you have to see it from his point of view. When a competitor moves in so close and fast into his territory, and he's in the right mood, the chances of him coming to check you out (or knock you out), can be very good. Nothing is ever a "gimme" with this, but an aggressive approach has proved far more successful for me than sitting and waiting for him to come in from 300 yards away.

We were just over the ridge into what is usually thicker cover, and I slowed my pace as I estimated that the bull was within 100 yards. I set up by a tree that had some good shooting lanes and Dave bugled again, and the bull responded with another loud scream that he finished off with chuckles. Now I knew almost exactly how close he was, so I took the risk to move another thirty yards closer and we set up again. I strained to get a look at him in the thick forest and I tried to focus on the farthest distances I could see. It's easy to have a habit of looking only 30-50 yards into the forest; you have to train your eyes to look farther, to focus on the most distant openings that you have available. I felt like I was right in his bedroom, but I couldn't see even a flicker of tan or a glimpse of an antler tine.

David was anxiously sitting about 50 yards above me and I motioned for him to scrape the tree with a branch, but he got the wrong message and he cow called a couple of times instead. I motioned again to scrap the tree, this time he got the right message and immediately found a good branch to start imitating an aggressive bull rubbing a tree. The bull responded with an aggressive scream and it sounded to me like he had cut the distance and was moving closer. I don't know what my heart rate was at that time, but I'm pretty sure my blood was flowing a lot faster than normal. I spent the time slowing my breathing and telling myself to keep it together.

Then the clock seemed to go into slow motion and in my mind I was getting concerned that we had lost the bull's attention. I would guess that we had been calling for at least twenty to twenty five minutes, and the thought that hit my mind was, "Don't let him get bored!"

Bulls love to "hang up" at distances they are no longer comfortable with and they seem to get bored when the activity slows. Because it seemed like everything had slowed and the bull was being quiet, I started to worry a little that maybe we needed to be even more aggressive. But something inside me said "Be patient!" so I used the time to try to focus on any small colors or movements that seemed to stand out just a little in the forest.

A few minutes later, I suddenly spotted the bull moving uphill about 60 yards away. My gun was on the wrong side of the tree I was sitting behind, but there wasn't time for a shot anyway. Just one glance at his body communicated two words to my mind, "He's big!" I could see his long, heavy antlers sweeping back toward his rump. I would love to have had a picture of my eyes at that point because they must have been the size of quarters! So I said the most common prayer in the world, "Help me!" and began looking for a shooting lane in the direction he was headed.

The thermals were definitely moving straight up, and that's where the best shooting lane was, but I didn't want to take the chance of him getting my scent. So I started looking for a secondary opening while watching for the bull to appear. It's amazing how fast a big animal like this can react to his nose, spin around, and get his body moving in the opposite direction! I didn't want to see that happen!

Suddenly I saw his head and antlers move through the thick trees less than forty yards away. That was about the longest distance I could see in that direction because of the thick brush.

During that previous summer whenever I took my gun out to shoot it, which was about four times spread out over three months, I would practice for free hand shooting. Sometimes loaded and actually firing, sometimes just using a primer, sometimes totally unloaded. But because you never know what kind of a shot you are going to get, I wanted to feel ready for a quick free-hand shot in thick cover to make sure I wouldn't flinch. As it turned out, that was exactly what I was going to get, a free-hand shot.

I leaned my elbow against the tree to steady my arm as the clock was rushing toward 12:34 p.m. and suddenly the bull's head and front shoulder were disappearing through the two-foot opening. I had wanted to shoot him in the front shoulder so he would go right down, but it was too late for that. I steadied the front sight right behind the front shoulder, held steady and squeezed. Smoke filled the air while the bull spun and crashed through the brush and out of sight.

The next thing I knew, David was running excitedly down toward me wanting to know more information. He hadn't seen the bull at all, even though the bull had climbed to about his same level of elevation and was headed in his direction. He was really shaking and holding up a video camera, which is not a good combination. He said he had seen me holding up my gun and that's when he lost control of his nerves. He also had to show me how he had scraped up his hands while he was rubbing the tree with several branches that could not take the strain of his aggression and suddenly broke in half. From experience I can easily say that calling in a bull is a very exciting and rewarding part of a hunt, and that was certainly confirmed in David's voice and intensity.

I was too excited to retell my story for him so I summed it all up in two little words, "He's big!" We slowly moved up to where the bull had been walking when I shot, we were looking for blood or tracks, but we couldn't locate either. Usually a bull's hooves will leave some pretty deep ruts in the ground, but we only found one small track, so we tried to find a dry log to sit on and wait for an hour before doing anymore tracking.

It takes a big bull time to expire; you do not want to rush this pursuit. It's hard to just sit and wait when in your mind he's getting away, but the smart thing to do is to wait an hour, then proceed slowly and let the sign you find dictate your tracking speed. If you see a lot of blood you can obviously proceed faster, little or no blood and you have to slow everything down.

After we had waited about five minutes, we suddenly heard the bull crashing into logs and rocks down below us. It sounded like a small herd of elk busting through the timber, but it was only one bull stumbling and falling. That was a beautiful sound to us especially since we couldn't find a drop of blood. Then, a strong thermal updraft brought the strong, pungent odor of a rutting bull right to our noses, and I pointed down the mountain and told David, "He's got to be right there!" But we still waited a full forty five minutes before moving down to try to find him.

We spread out about fifty yards apart and slowly moved down toward what we had heard and smelled. About 100 yards down and David called me over and pointed down about another 50 yards. With my binoculars I could easily see the huge tan colored body of the bull on the ground. As we excitedly moved closer, we could see his huge antlers sticking up high over his head. I turned and gave my son a big high five before excitedly covering the remaining distance. All either of us could say was, "He's huge!"

David kept repeating the words, "Oh Mylanta! He's huge!" As we stood over our prize, overwhelmed with how everything had happened so suddenly and how large the bull was, I couldn't help but stop to thank David for doing a great job of calling. He certainly had proven himself to be an excellent caller.

This was the culmination of about 32 years of hunting elk for me. Since David could legally buy a tag, I had been bringing him to these mountains to teach and train him in hunting these beautiful animals, and we had just collected a dividend check that was bigger than anything we could have imagined.

The bull grossed 344 4/8 inches, with a net score of 338 4/8 inches. Bob, who raises steers and is very accustomed to their weight, guessed that this bull was over 900 pounds. A father-son team successfully taking Boone and Crocket bulls on the first day of season, two years in a row on public land!

I felt overwhelmed with gratitude and pride in what we had accomplished together and how much God had blessed us. To me, this was more than just a hunting trip, this was "As Good as it Gets" for a hunter.

See "Think It Through" – page 92

15 THINK IT THROUGH...

The following pages are designed to help you work through the main topic of each chapter. If you are reading through the book alone, I suggest you write down some of your main thoughts, get a Bible and look up the passages that I've listed, and even follow through with the closing application. Just as you would invest some time into planning a hunt to help make it successful, five or ten minutes dedicated to learning something new to improve your life is a worthy investment.

If you are reading through the book as part of a group study, I suggest you keep the group to less than twelve and take the time to let everybody recall and share something in the opening thoughts. Let volunteers read the scripture passages rather than putting pressure on those who are not comfortable reading to a group. Give everybody time to think through the questions and respond. The "Application" may be the most important part of the discussion so I urge everybody to briefly write down their decision and seriously follow through. The next time you meet the first thing you do together could be to share the results. Don't forget to have fun and embellish your own hunting stories with humor and intrigue.

CHAPTER 1 REFLECTION:

1. Think about a big disappointment you experienced as a sportsman.

2. What do you think the lesson they'd "never forget" was?

SCRIPTURE INSIGHT:

1. Read Job 6:14-21—Describe the disappointment Job was facing. ______________________________.

2. What is the root cause of disappointment and what elements heighten its affects on us? ______________________________.

3. Read Jeremiah 2:36-37—Why is God allowing his people to become disappointed? ______________________________.

4. How does the Lord turn disappointment around to work for our good? ______________________________.

5. Read Romans 8:28—"All things work together for good..." Why? ______________________________.

6. Recall a disappointment you've experienced that God worked for your good. ______________________________.

7. Describe your current relationship with Jesus Christ and how disappointment has affected it. ______________________________.

APPLICATION:

1. My plan for dealing with disappointment in the future is: ______________________________.

2. Ask the Lord for courage and wisdom in dealing with a current disappointment.

***

CHAPTER 2 REFLECTION:

1. What were the uniting factors in our hunting effort?

2. What difference did a team effort make in our hunt?

SCRIPTURE INSIGHT:

1. Read 2 Chronicles 20:1-23—Describe how a team effort won the day for this community: ______________________________.

2. What might have happened had each person tried to do it alone? ______________________________.

3. According to verse 23, why were their enemies defeated? ______________ ______________________________.

4. Read Ephesians 4:1-3—These verses list several characteristics that are required for any team to work well. What are they, and what differences will each one make? ______________________________ ______________________________.

APPLICATION:

1. Read Colossians 3:12-17—List the characteristics Paul tells us to clothe ourselves with. How could each contribute to your group or team? ______________________________ ______________________________.

2. Write down at least one characteristic that you need to "clothe" yourself with to be a better team player. ______________________________ ______________________________.

3. Take a few minutes to pray, asking God to help you to become a better team player.

***

CHAPTER 3 REFLECTION:

1. Recall a time when you felt confused about your circumstances and what you should do. Why is it so easy to make a mistake when you're in this position? ______________________________.

2. "I just couldn't give the search up." What should we do when we feel something this deeply? Why? ______________________________.

SCRIPTURE INSIGHT:

1. Read James 5:16b-18 and 1 Kings 18:36-46—What kind of guy was Elijah? Do you think Elijah was winging it? ______________________.

2. What does this story teach us about prayer? The power of prayer? A believer's authority in prayer? Perseverance? ______________________.

3. Read Luke 11:1-10—In verses 2-4, Jesus is teaching more about some principles of prayer than prescribing a formal prayer for recitation. What are the six main principles?

   ____

   ____.

4. In verse 8 Jesus gives the reason why the man's need was met. This word is also translated "shamelessness." What kind of a word picture does that give you? ______________________________.

5. Read Proverbs 3:5-6—Why does God make the "paths" for the man who trusts and acknowledges Him "straight?" Define "straight." Give a personal example. ______________________________

APPLICATION:

1. What do you need guidance for right now? ______________________.

2. Pray for God's guidance in your life.

***

CHAPTER 4 REFLECTION:

1. Recall a hunting related conflict you were involved in. What are some of the common causes of conflict?

2. What are the best ways to diffuse someone's anger? What about your anger?

3. How do you feel when someone apologizes to you directly, but tries to minimize their offence? How about when they accept total responsibility?

SCRIPTURE INSIGHT:

1. Read Acts 15:36-41—Why was there a conflict? How was it resolved? ____

2. How did the Lord use this conflict for good? What are some positive sides to conflict? ____

3. What do the following verses tell us: Colossians 4:10; 2 Timothy 4:11; Philemon 1:23-24; Colossians 3:12-13? ____________________ ____.

4. What conflict resolution principles do you see in these wisdom verses from Proverbs? 10:19; 12:16; 13:3; 15:1,4,18,31; 16:28,32; 17:1,14; 18:13; 19:11; 22:24-25; 24:28-29; 25:21-22; 26:20. ____________________ ____ ____.

APPLICATION:

1. If you are in an unresolved conflict situation currently, what can you do to resolve it? ____.

2. Ask for the Lord's help in resolving conflict.

***

CHAPTER 5 REFLECTION:

1. Recall a hunt when you or someone you were with gave up too soon.

2. How do you think Paul kept going when the odds of success seemed so small?

SCRIPTURE INSIGHT:

1. Read 1 Timothy 4:15-16 and Hebrews 10:36—What does the Bible say are the rewards of perseverance? Why is it so important? ______________________________.

2. What two areas does the Apostle Paul say we need to watch? Why? ______________________________.

3. Does the "wili of God" for our lives often require perseverance? Why? ______________________________.

4. Read Romans 5:3-5 and James 1:2-4—Just as climbing a mountain produces physical muscle, what do times of testing or trials produce? How are we to face them? ______________________________.

5. Read Hebrews 12:1—Things that "hinder" and "the sin that so easily entangles" are opposed to spiritual growth and perseverance in our lives. Why? See also 2 Peter 1:5-9. ______________________________ ______________________________.

APPLICATION:

1. What area of your spiritual life needs some perseverance today? ______________________________.

2. Pray about the area(s) of your relationship with Christ you need to persevere in. ______________________________.

***

CHAPTER 6 REFLECTION:

1. Recall a hunt when you successfully called in a game animal/bird.

2. In what ways are the calling strategies we used with bull elk similar to temptations you face with sin?

3. Why do you think some bulls are so quick to respond to a caller, and how does that relate to our responses to some temptations?

SCRIPTURE INSIGHT:

1. Read James 1:12-15—Why will the man who perseveres be blessed? ____.

2. How does temptation begin? How does it progress? How is James suggesting we can overcome it? ____________________ ____.

3. Read 1 Corinthians 10:13—How has God provided "a way out" for you in temptations you've faced? __________________________.

4. Read Matthew 4:1-10—What three things was Jesus tempted with? How did he defeat each one? ________________________ ____.

5. Read Romans 6:11-14—How does Paul say we can overcome sin? ____.

APPLICATION:

1. What scriptures do I need to apply to my life and temptations right now? ____.

2. Ask the Lord to show you the way out of a temptation with which you are struggling.

***

CHAPTER 7 REFLECTION:

1. Recall a memory of when you were a part of a team that accomplished something outstanding.

2. Why do you think the successful trio was so willing to endure and even laugh at the difficulties they were facing?

3. What dynamics make fellowship work?

SCRIPTURE INSIGHT:

1. 1 Corinthians 1:9—This is a very special fellowship; how do we enter into it? Ephesians 2:1-10; Romans 10:9-11 ____.

2. Read 1 John 1:6—What does this fellowship require? ______________.

3. Read Philippians 3:10—Describe what the "fellowship of sharing in his suffering" may include. ______________________________.

4. Read 1 John 1:3, 7—What things contribute to the fellowship John is describing? ______________________________.

APPLICATION:

1. What do I need to do to increase my fellowship with Christ? ______________________________.

2. What fellowship could I become a part of? Or, what does my current fellowship need me to contribute right now? ______________________________.

***

CHAPTER 8 REFLECTION:

1. Recall a story of when you or someone you know experienced an unusual healing.

2. How did we know for sure that Ross had indeed received a healing from the Lord? How did Ross' sense of release help his faith?

3. Do most of us only expect God to heal or deliver us at church? When and where should we expect an answer?
4. Could Carroll's healing have been coincidence? Why?

SCRIPTURE INSIGHT:
1. Read Ephesians 3:14-21—What did the Apostle Paul pray for? When was/is this prayer answered? ______________________________
____.

2. Read James 5:13-18—What does James say will result in healing? Who should pray? ______________________________.

3. Why does he use Elijah as an example? (See 1 Kings 17:19-29; 18:41-45)
____.

4. Read Mark 1:40-42—Why does Jesus heal? Do these things change over time? ______________________________.

5. Read Mark 6:2-6—Why couldn't Jesus heal many in His own town? How do we apply this to our own situation? (See Mark 11:20-25; 16:15-18).
____
____.

APPLICATION:
1. Who do you know who needs healing? Pray for them now. __________.

2. Who could you go see, spend some time with, or pray for that is in a physical need? ______________________________.

***

CHAPTER 9 REFLECTION:

1. Recall a time when you were desperate for direction in your life or you were trying to help someone else that was.

2. None of us likes the feeling that our situation requires more than we can handle. What is good about being in that position?

3. How would you define faith for someone who doesn't believe in God?

SCRIPTURE INSIGHT:

1. Read Hebrews 11:1-3, 8, 11-12—In your own words, how does the Bible define faith? Why does it take faith to understand that God formed the universe?____
____.

2. What was so significant about what Abraham did in verse 8? Verse 11-12? ____.

3. Read 1 Corinthians 16:13-14—What characteristics do these verses say should be combined with faith? Why? __________________________.

4. Read Ephesians 2:8-10—How does faith affect works? What does Paul say is our purpose in life? ____________________________________
____.

5. Read Ephesians 3:12-19—How does faith help us in prayer? Define "freedom" and "confidence."_________________________________
____.

APPLICATION:

1. What changes need to happen in your faith?

2. Using your new knowledge and faith, pray for the direction and needs in your life and of others you know. You might pray with someone else also.

***

CHAPTER 10 REFLECTION:

1. Recall a personal experience of when something very small spoiled success for you.

2. How does it feel to be defeated by a little detail when you've succeeded in getting all the big things right?

3. What kinds of little things affect your relationships?

SCRIPTURE INSIGHT:

1. Read Song of Solomon 2:15— What kinds of potentially destructive "little foxes" might he be talking about? (also see Ephesians 5:22-33; 1 Peter 3:1-9).____

   ____.

2. If you are married, share one or two "little foxes" that you and your spouse have struggled with. ______________________________.

3. How did you "catch" them? ______________________________.

4. There are also "little foxes" that are trying to ruin your relationship with Christ. Can you list some of them? (Also see Galatians 5:19-21; Ephesians 4:17-5:7). ____________________________________

   ____.

5. Read Romans 8. The Apostle Paul lists several ways to capture the "little foxes" in our lives. Name several. ______________________________

   ____.

APPLICATION:

1. Think about how you can begin to put some of these to work today. ____.

2. Ask the Lord to help you to apply these to your life.

***

CHAPTER 11 REFLECTION:

1. How would you define compromise? Share an experience when a compromise you made resulted in an unfavorable result. How do you think Bob felt when his gun failed to fire?

2. What kinds of compromises do we make spiritually? Morally? Ethically?

3. Why was my decision to buy a side lock rifle a compromise?

SCRIPTURE INSIGHT:

1. Read Revelation 2:12-17—These believers have been faithful, yet they compromised? How? ______________________________.

2. Read Numbers 25:1-3; 31:16; Jude 11- What can we learn from this? ____ ________.

3. Read 1 Corinthians 6:12, 19-20—What principles does Paul say he follows when it comes to questionable practices? ______________ ____.

4. Read Genesis 39:2-12—How did Joseph handle his temptations to compromise? Does our society bait or honor men like Joseph? Why? ____ ____.

APPLICATION:

1. Write down one or two areas you are tempted to compromise in: ____.

2. Think about ways you can become accountable for your choices. Spend some time praying for help. ______________________________.

***

CHAPTER 12 REFLECTION:

1. Recall an experience when you felt like God had blessed a hunting or fishing trip. Check out John 21:4-11.

2. How could selfishness ruin a hunt or fishing trip?

3. Why do you think selfishness and criticism are related?

SCRIPTURE INSIGHT:

1. Read Philippians 2:3-4—Why is "selfish ambition" the mortal enemy of unity or teamwork? ______________________________________.

2. How could "consider others better than yourselves," eliminate selfishness from your life? How about looking out for, "the interests of others?" ______________________________________
______________________________________.

3. Read 1 Samuel 23:17-18—What phrase does Jonathan, the king's son, use with David that describes him as a selfless and giving man? ______________________________________.

4. Jonathan and David made a covenant together. How is this an act of selflessness? How could they trust each other? ____________________
______________________________________.

5. Read 1 Samuel 24—Describe David's acts of selflessness. ________
______________________________________.

APPLICATION:

1. In what relationships are you exhibiting selfishness? ________________.

2. What could you change so that God's blessing could be released in your life? ______________________________________.

3. Pray, asking God to enable you to become a selfless person.

***

CHAPTER 13 REFLECTION:

1. What are some goals that you have met in your hunting experiences? Name one current goal that you have. What is one hunting goal you have for a family member?

2. If someone asked you "What really drives you?" what would you say?

SCRIPTURE INSIGHT:

1. Describe the goal in each of these passages: 2 Corinthians 5:9; Philippians 3:13-14; 1 Peter 1:7-9. ____ ____.

2. Read 1 Timothy 1:3-7—What does the writer warn against? How easy is it to spend our time and attention on things that, in the long run, do more harm than good? What should we spend our time and attention on? ____ ____.

3. Read Luke 13:31-32—What was Jesus' goal in this passage? (see John 2:4, 7:30, 8:20, 13:1, 17:1; 19:30; 1 Peter 1:20; Revelation 13:8). What does this goal mean to you? How would your biggest goals compare with His? Who was the "fox"? What were his goals? (Verse 31; Luke 23:8-12; Acts 2:23-24, 3:13-18) How did God over ride Herod's goals for His own purpose? ____ ____.

APPLICATION:

1. Read 2 Corinthians 5:9 again and describe what new goals He may be challenging you to set for yourself? How about some new hunting goals? Family goals? ____ ____.

2. What should the ultimate goal for your life become? ________________.

***

CHAPTER 14 REFLECTION:

1. What was one of the best hunting trips you've ever had? What made it the best? What could have made it even better?

SCRIPTURE INSIGHT:

1. Who was the very first hunter in the Bible? (Genesis 3:21) Why did he hunt? (Genesis 3:1-10) What does that tell you about him? (Genesis 3:14-15; 1 Corinthians 15:20-26; Romans 16:20). ________________
____.

2. Read Genesis 25:21-34—Esau loved hunting and he might have been a great hunter, but there were some things missing or out of order in his life. What were they? What can happen when we put an over emphasis on hunting or hobbies? ________________
____.

3. Read 1 Samuel 17:32-37—David was a great hunter, what made him great? What motivated him to hunt? How did it help him succeed in life and relationships? ________________
____.

APPLICATION:

1. If you asked your wife or children how balanced your time is between hunting and sports activities and spending time with them, what would they say? What about your financial spending? ________________
____
____.

2. How could hunting and the sports activities you love become beneficial for everyone in your family? For other relationships?
3. What story would you like your legacy to tell? What needs to change for that to happen? ________________
____.

***

APPENDIX #1— 44 ELK HUNTING TIPS

1. You can shoot an elk from anywhere except the inside your tent. Get up early and get moving!
2. High pitch bugles and cow calls are better. Keep it simple. Short. Soft. Imitate the bugle you hear.
3. Check patches of dense timber up high on the north side.
4. Size and depth of wallow indicates amount of use. Clearness of water indicates when last used.
5. ½ - ¾ distance up the mountain in elevation is often best. Get ahead of them.
6. Noon hunt/calling is limited to bedding areas
7. Call from above or the same level of elevation.
8. Watch the wind!
9. An increase in bugling tempo means he has a cow in heat. Other bulls will come to see.
10. Satellite bulls often come quietly so they don't attract attention of herd bulls. Herd bulls often move the cows away from challenging bulls.
11. Find a bedding area, get above it and call. Bedded elk spread out. Bulls are often not alone.
12. Hunt until the last minute of light and keep a positive attitude.
13. Bulls often grunt without bugling and they'll respond to a grunt or tree thrashing when they won't respond to a bugle.
14. Spikes often have high pitched, short bugles.
15. A herd bull won't go far from his cows for long, about 300 yards.
16. With archery, be in front of trees, brush, etc. w/ good camouflage.
17. Blow cow call softly as you are moving, blow 2-4 times in a row and wait 5 minutes. Sound like a mini-herd.
18. Watching trails is usually futile.
19. If bulls move away, pursue them w/ a bugle. Increase the intensity as you get closer. Thrash brush & break branches, be aggressive.
20. Find fresh rubs, set up and bugle.
21. Don't call from roads. You are only educating the elk to your presence.
22. Call frequently (every 15 minutes). Don't be timid.
23. The aggressive approach is best early in the season, before hunting pressure begins.
24. Get w/in 50 yards if possible in heavy timber before bugling again. Watch the wind!
25. Two return bugles tell you he's listening, so move quickly! If he retreats, follow closely and confront him. Bugling is not a lure.
26. Herd bull will have cows in his area and will be seeking cows, so use cow call. Use a hyper-cow call. Call every 5-10 seconds.

27. With a herd bull, penetrate the herd and bugle or get a shooter ahead of them.
28. If he's raking antlers, move in quickly or rake your own tree.
29. Use a softer approach w/ younger or ruffed up bulls; cow call in between, use soft, high pitched, single note squeal or just "eucks" or short bugles or just rub.
30. Noise is not a problem when you are in a hot pursuit.
31. They're closer than you think, especially if you can hear the grunt, chirp or glug-glug sound.
32. "Glug-glug" is the sound of a bull herding cows, two notes in throat as if gulping water.
33. 2 yr. olds have a high-pitched bugle, rarely roar.
34. Older bulls rut earlier (Aug. to early Sept.) and respond earlier to bugling. Bulls most likely to respond to cow calls in peak are satellites. Satellites are most aggressive in middle to late September, which is also the best success time at getting all ages to respond to bull & cow calls.
35. Locate bulls w/ a high-pitched, single note bugle w/out roar or grunt. If you are not sure of size of a bull- use small bull bugle.
36. Be patient. Generally bugle once, than wait. Give each location at least fifteen minutes- Wait long enough. Don't call too often if bull is close. Follow the bull's tempo. Don't set up where there's no cover, bulls want to stay in the heaviest cover they can. Watch for more than one bull. Listen for silent bulls.
37. Carry estrus urine and use it a lot, especially when setting up and calling.
38. Set up before you bugle.
39. Give a bull some time. Be persistent if sign is good. Be the aggressor—move in on him QUICKLY.
40. Don't sit in camp during wet weather.
41. Assume you'll call in a bull on every attempt.
42. Excite the bull, stir him up, and don't let him get bored. Add natural pauses. The closer you get the more likely he'll come in. If hung up, bugle away from you or move away from the elk. Put the shooter at least 50-100 yards in front.
43. If he circles downwind, you circle downwind fast. Spray elk urine on the cover around you.
44. Push and irritate a bull until he gets mad. Stalk a herd bull— have a partner bugle from behind while you stalk in quietly. Or get ahead of him, or get close and bugle aggressively.

APPENDIX #2—Gear Packing List

Everything you'll need:

- [ ] Wind Detector
- [ ] Camp Shoes & Jacket
- [ ] Safety Certificate
- [ ] Water Purifying Tablets/ Filter
- [ ] License
- [ ] Lantern & Fuel(1 Quart); Extra Mantles
- [ ] Knife, Steel, Bone Saw
- [ ] Plate, Cup, Plastic utensils
- [ ] First Aid W/Aspirin & Ibuprofen
- [ ] Aluminum Fry Pan, Lg. Pot for boiling water
- [ ] Lg. Spoon
- [ ] ______________________________
- [ ] Shovel
- [ ] Rain Gear & Emergency Kits
- [ ] Hip Boots (If needed for packing in)
- [ ] (6) Lg. Heavy Garbage Bags
- [ ] (4) Heavy Plastic Bags 3 Mil.+
- [ ] Tent, Tarp & Rope
- [ ] Water Containers (Collapsible) (3)
- [ ] Game Bags
- [ ] Coolers (at least 120 Cu. In./Elk for traveling home)
- [ ] Stove & Fuel
- [ ] Light Rope/Cord
- [ ] Elastic Band-Aid
- [ ] Two Way Radios
- [ ] Toilet Paper (1+)/Person
- [ ] Folding Chair

- ❑ Marking Tape
- ❑ Compass
- ❑ GPS & Batteries (2 Sets)
- ❑ (1) Paper Towel
- ❑ Washcloth, Towel (1)
- ❑ Shampoo, Tooth Paste/Brush
- ❑ Unscented body & face wipes (40)
- ❑ Scent Killer (1/4 Guys)
- ❑ Calls (Cow & Bull) Bugle Bands (1/Day)
- ❑ Scent & Spray Bottle (Archery)
- ❑ Light Gloves (2 Pair)
- ❑ Head Lamp; 1 Set Extra Batteries
- ❑ 1 Extra Flashlight
- ❑ Camo Gear (2-Pants+ 1 Rainproof), 2 Jackets (Light & Rain Jacket), Face Mask or Paint, Cap
- ❑ Orange Vest & Cap (Muzzleloader)
- ❑ Shoes & Socks (3 Wool, 3 Cotton)
- ❑ Clothes: 1 Change for Packing In, 4 Shirts, 3 Sets Polypro. Tops, 1 Bottom, 1/Day Underwear
- ❑ Gun & Ammo, Or Bow Etc.
- ❑ Fanny Pack
- ❑ Lg. Bag/ Frame/ (3) Bungee Cords
- ❑ Sleeping Bag, Mat & Cot
- ❑ Matches/ Lighters
- ❑ Binoculars or Range Finder
- ❑ Camera
- ❑ Bleach (Purify Water)
- ❑ Pillow, Sweats & Wool Socks
- ❑ Alarm Clock

- ❑ Food: (1) Loaf Bread (3-4 Slices/Day), Envelope Meats, Sardines, (2) Dried Fruit, Sm. Hard Candy to moisten your throat
    - Water (2) 32 Oz./Day, (6)/Day Hydrating Mix, (2)/Day Hot Drink Mixes
    - Trail Mix (¾ Lb.), (3)/Day Cereal Bars, Cereal (1), Dry Milk (1), ¼ Lb. Pop Corn & Oil, (3)/Day Cheese Crackers
    - Peanut Butter
    - Jerky ½ Gallon Bag (3-5 Lbs. pre-dried Meat)
    - Freeze Dried Suppers
    - ½ Lb. Butter, (3-4) Peppers, (2) Onions, Salt/Pepper
- ❑ Chap Stick
- ❑ Plastic Ground Cover
- ❑ Extra Pair of Shoes?

PHOTOS

Bull elk I encountered in Colorado.

Our hunt in Colorado starts here.

The eternal trail to camp!

September has to be the most beautiful time to hunt.

Elk live in very beautiful places.

My first bull.

The work is worth the rewards.

Teamwork pays big dividends. Dan, me, Ross, Paul & Mark.

Paul (on right) and me with our first bull.

Me, Ross, Paul, Randy and Dan.

Perseverance pays off.

Our famous "Bull Hill" is in the foreground.

Paul's 2001 bull.

Chad with his first bull.

Rodney's first bull in 2004.

Randy, David, Phil, Joel, and me.

Randy's 2004 bull.

Me, Bob, Ross, Chad, Joe and Paul.

Chad, Mark, Bob, Ross and me packing out my bull.

This bull redefined our need for guidance in trailing.

Phil with a bull his dad, Rod, called in for him on "Bull Hill."

My son David's last day archery cow in 2008.

Nathan's first bull, opening day 2010.

Nathan, his dad Paul, and Dr. Gary Kotecki.

Dave's first bull in 2011.

Me, David, Randy and Rodney.

Dave and me with his 318″ bull.

"Carry this uphill? No problem!"

Kyle's first bull in 2011.

My 2013 Opening day bull.

Dave and me with my 2013 bull, 244 4/8" gross.

Bob, Gary, me and David

Carroll, David and Kyle with Carroll's first bull in 2014

Just because it's hard work doesn't mean it can't be fun.

Don't let the hard work keep you from your adventure!

ABOUT THE AUTHOR

Paul N. Carlson was born in the central Minnesota town of Willmar where his dad instilled in him a love for hunting. He is a graduate of North Central University and became a pastor in 1981 when he and his wife Ruth moved to northeast Colorado. He has since spent time on staff in churches in Wyoming and Wisconsin. In 1985 they moved to a small town in northeast Wisconsin where Paul remains the Lead Pastor.

Paul's love for elk hunting and for the mountains elk live in fueled a desire to become successful in harvesting bulls the do-it-yourself way. This led him on an unplanned journey of over thirty years of learning to successfully hunt bull elk and pass on what he learned. He has called in numerous bulls on public land at close range for his hunting partners and mentored his son with this skill. His love for God and the outdoors combined to turn elk camps into spiritual retreats—and that's what led to the writing of this book.

You can contact the author at: "Guidetobuglingbulls.com."